Bridal
Floral Design

Transforming Wedding Bouquets into Colorful Masterpieces

Coloring Book

Crystal Moon

ISBN: 978-0-9888737-6-6

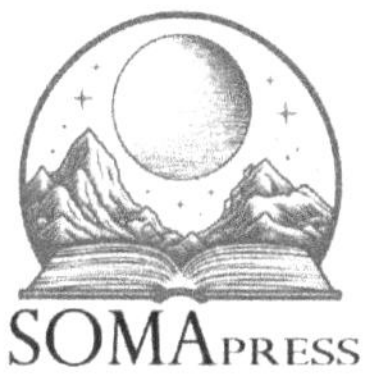

SOMA PRESS

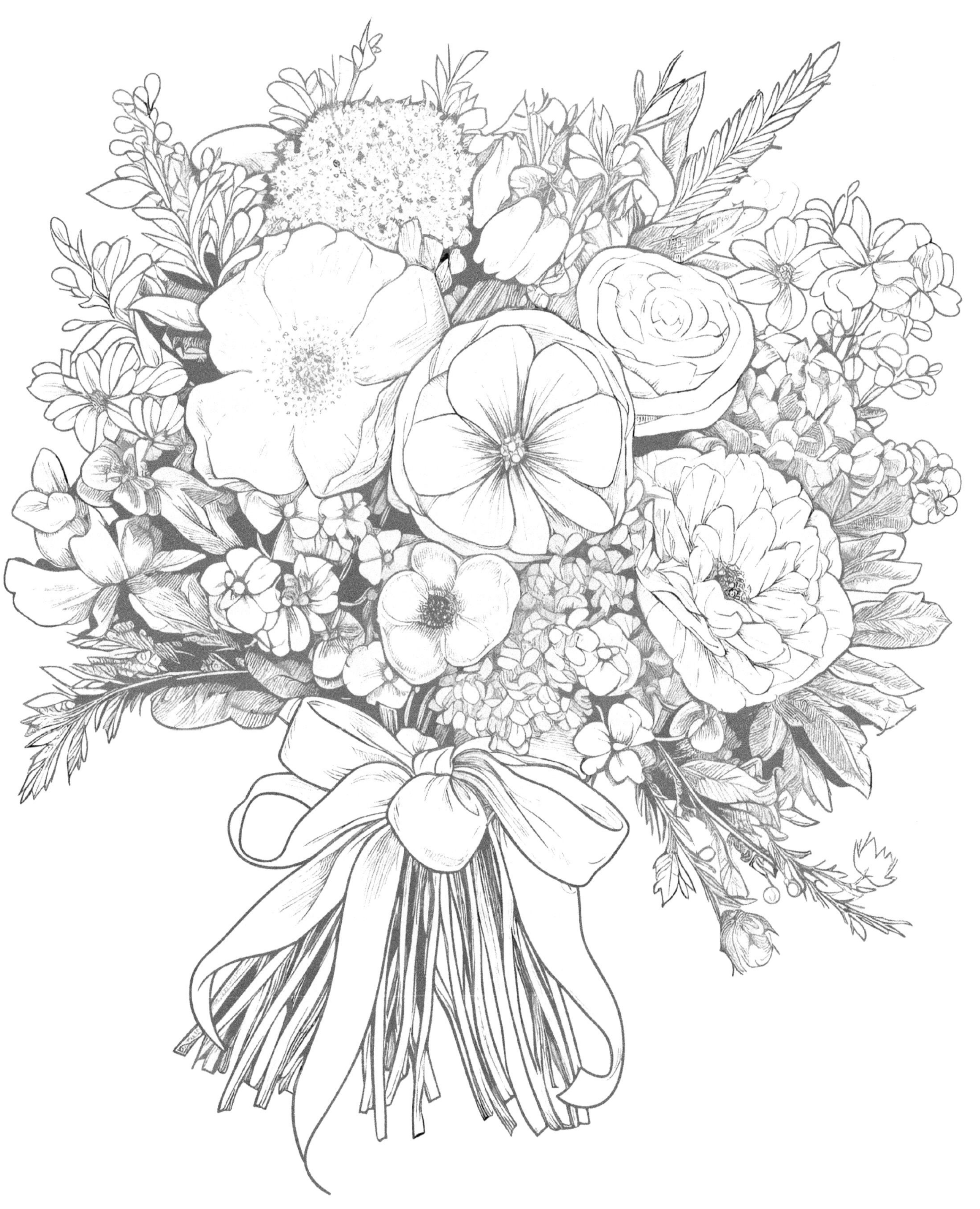

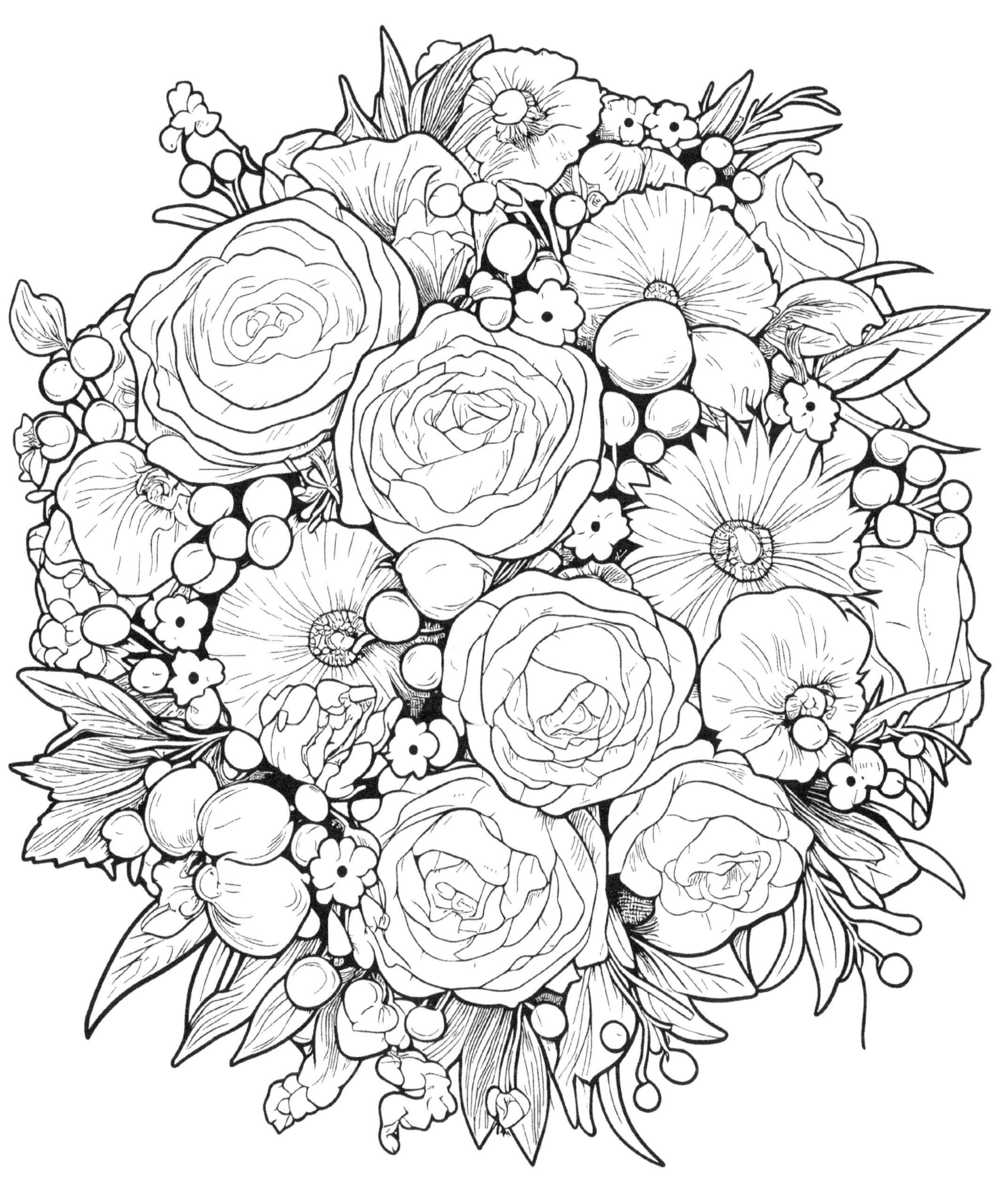

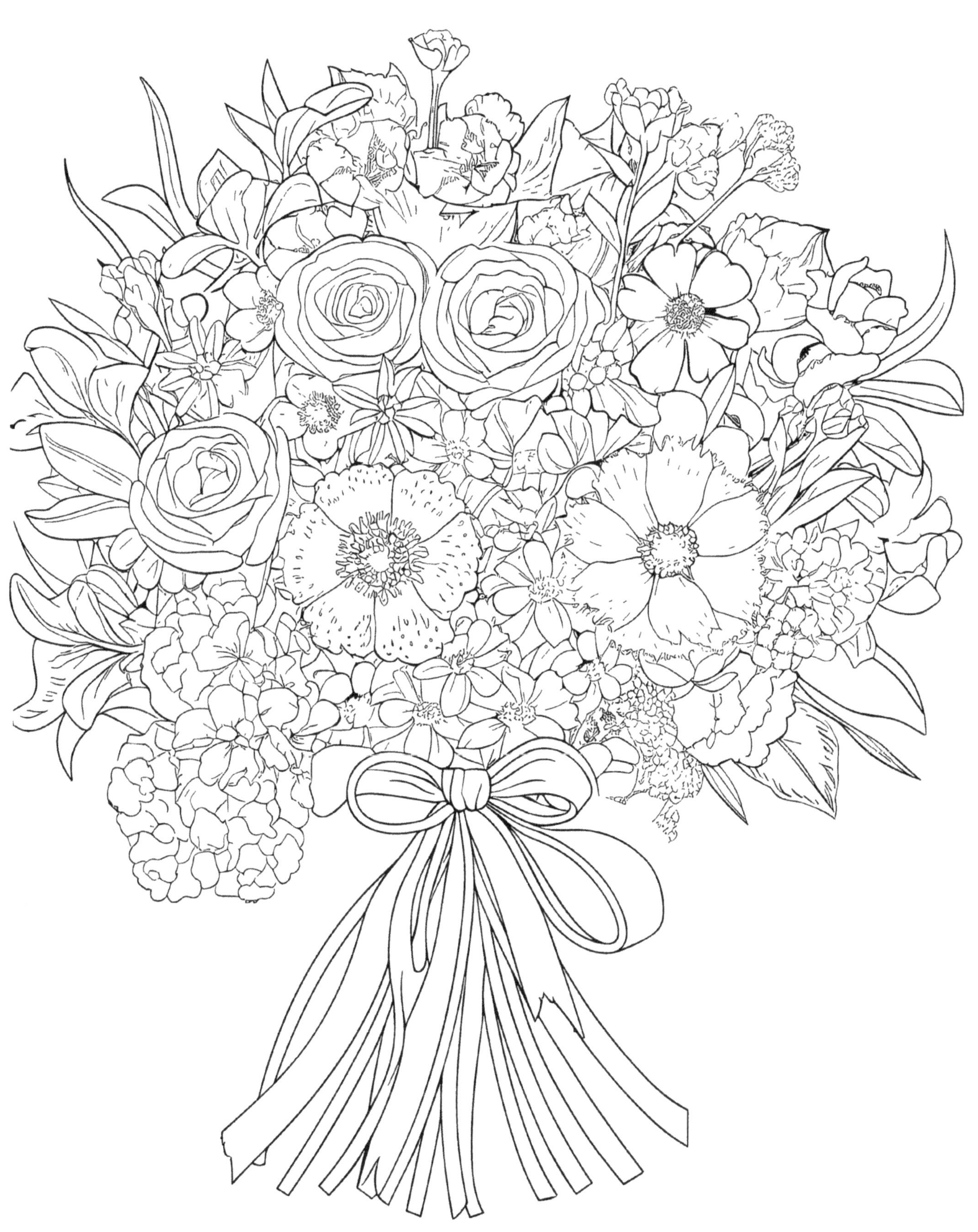

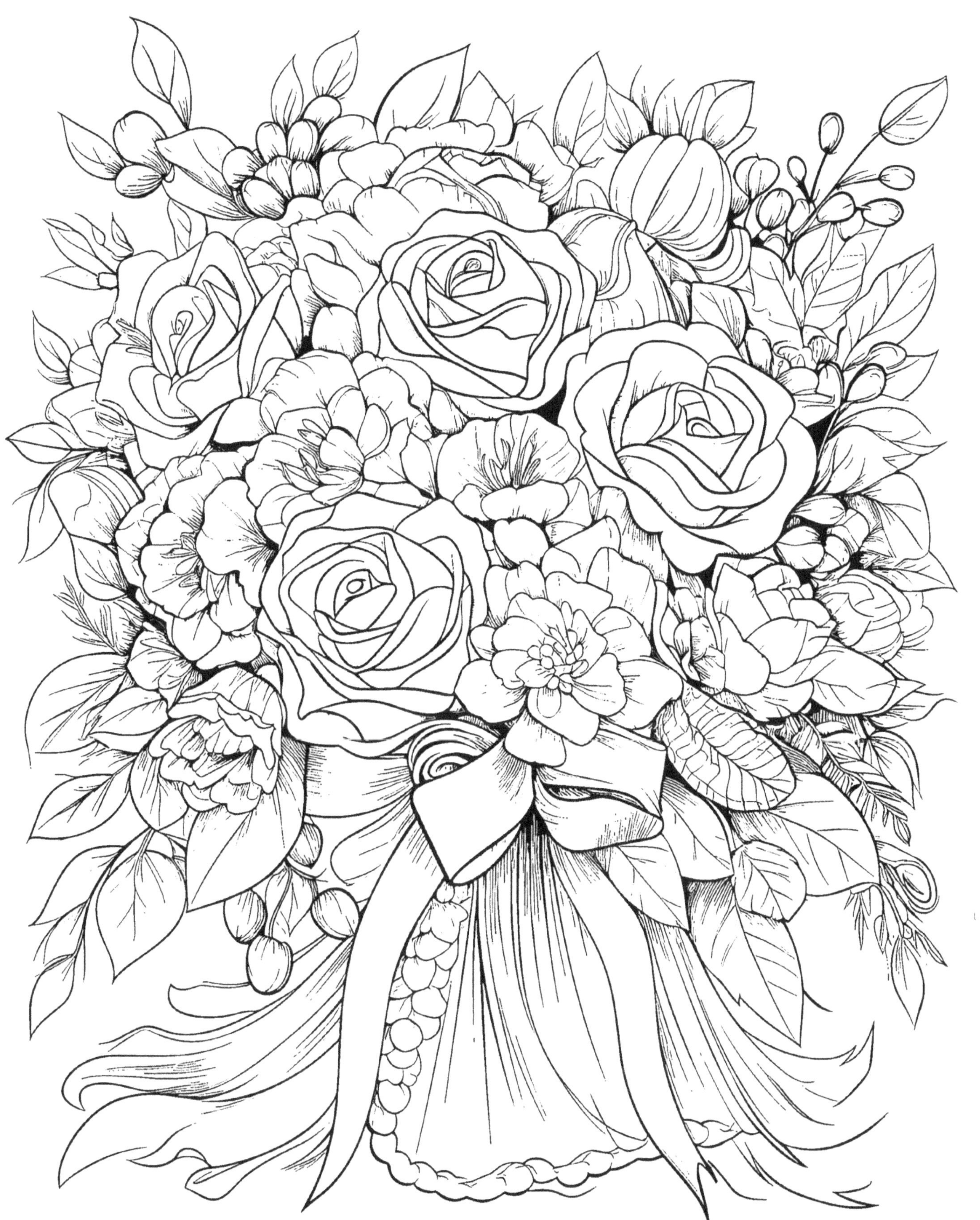

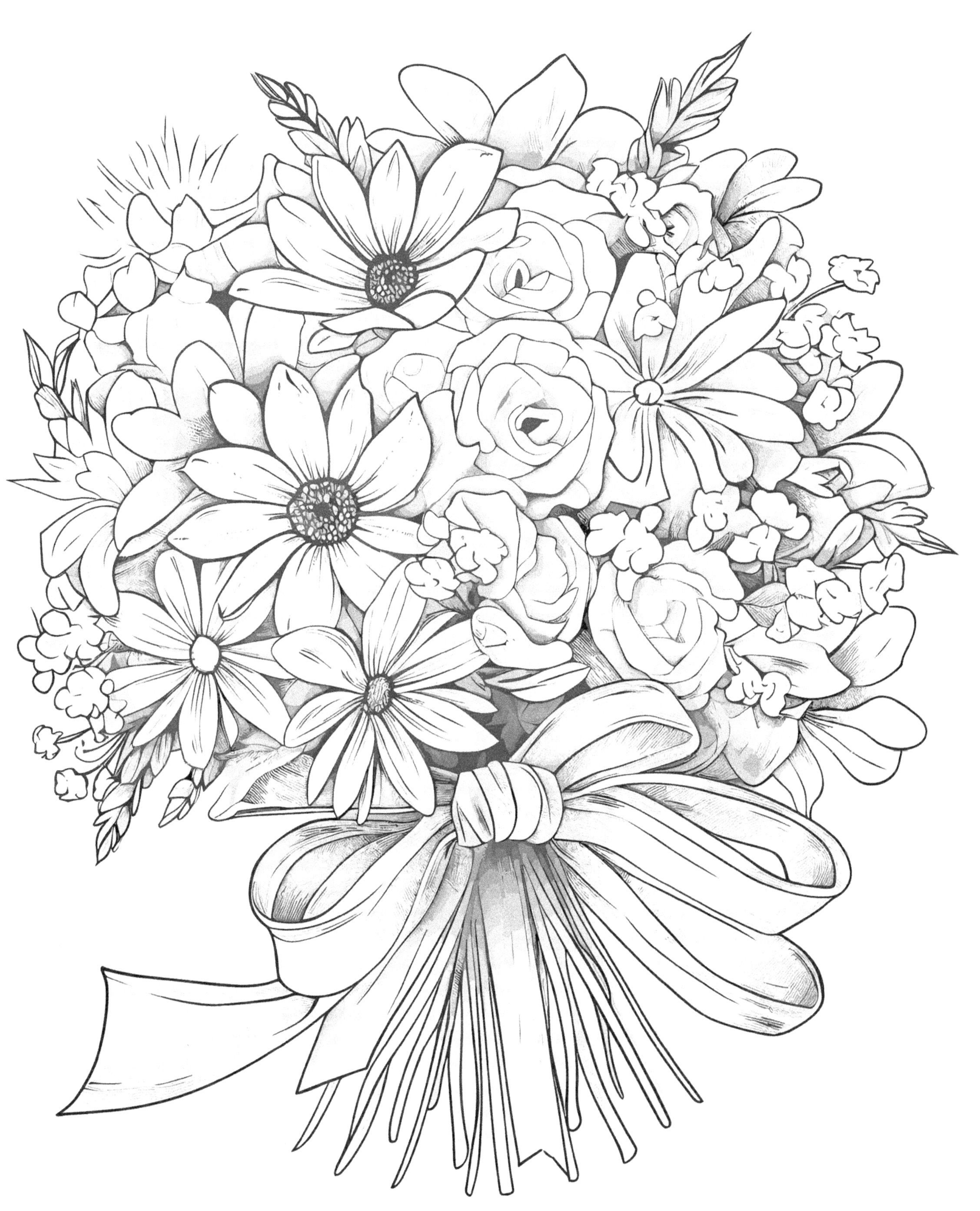

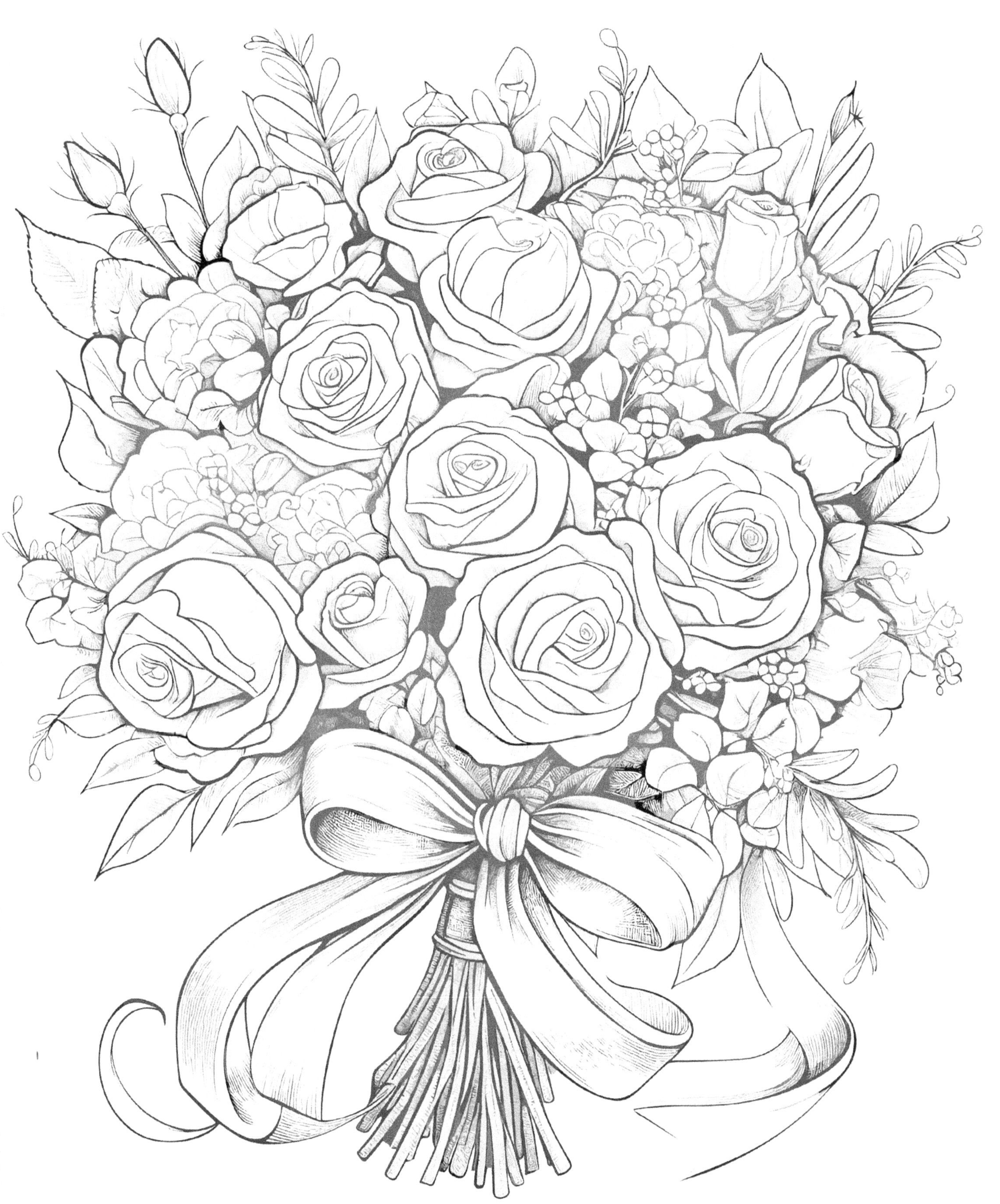

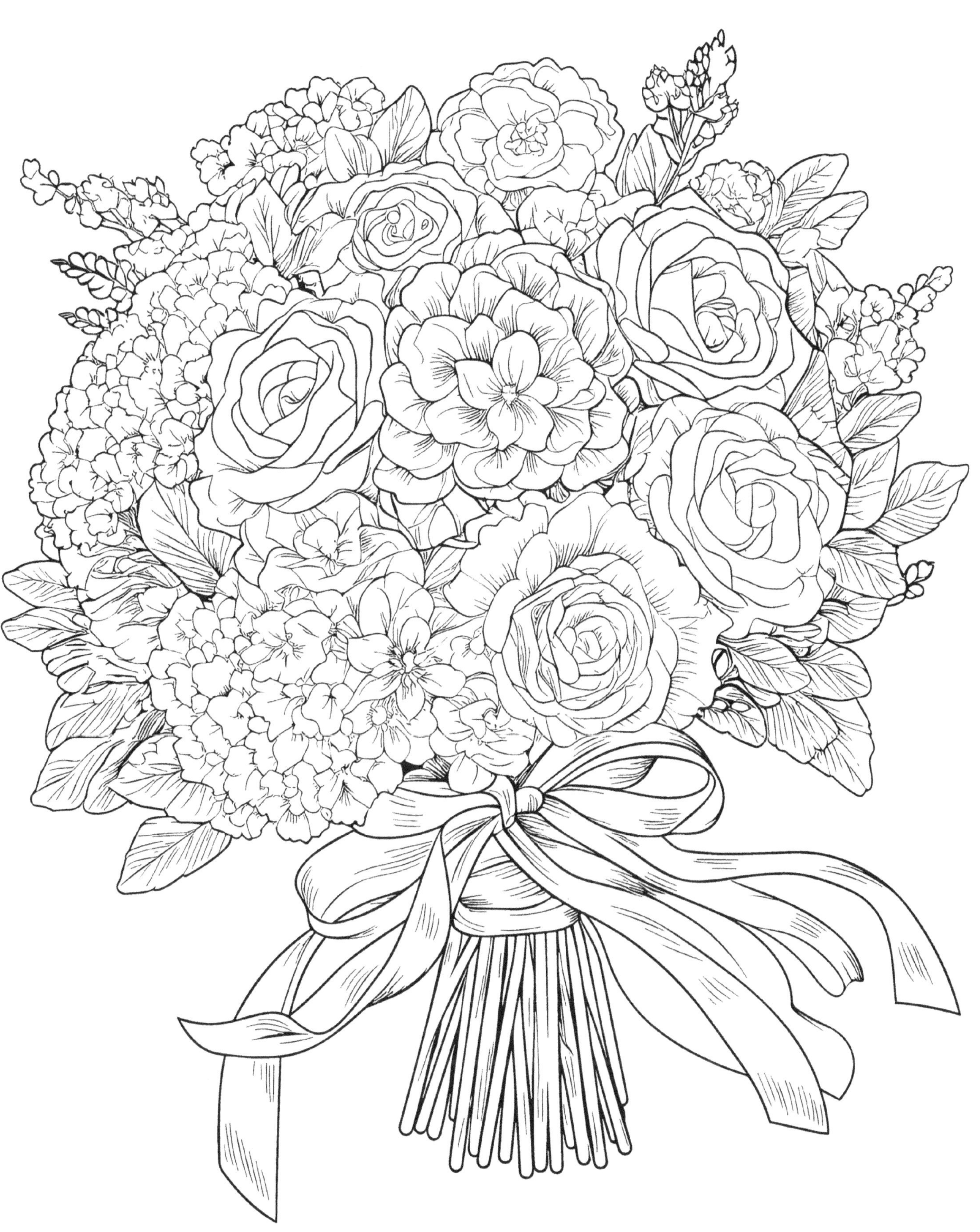

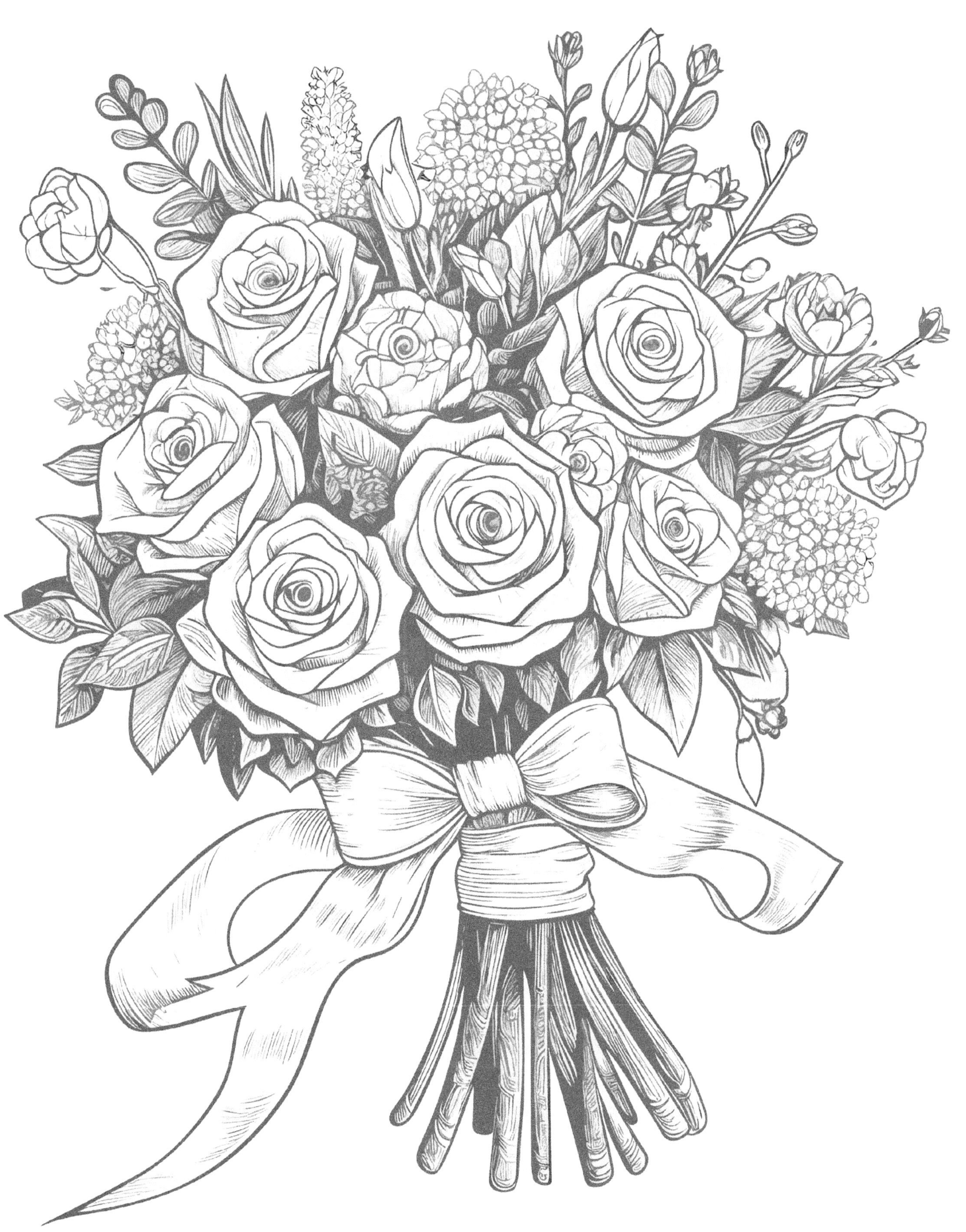

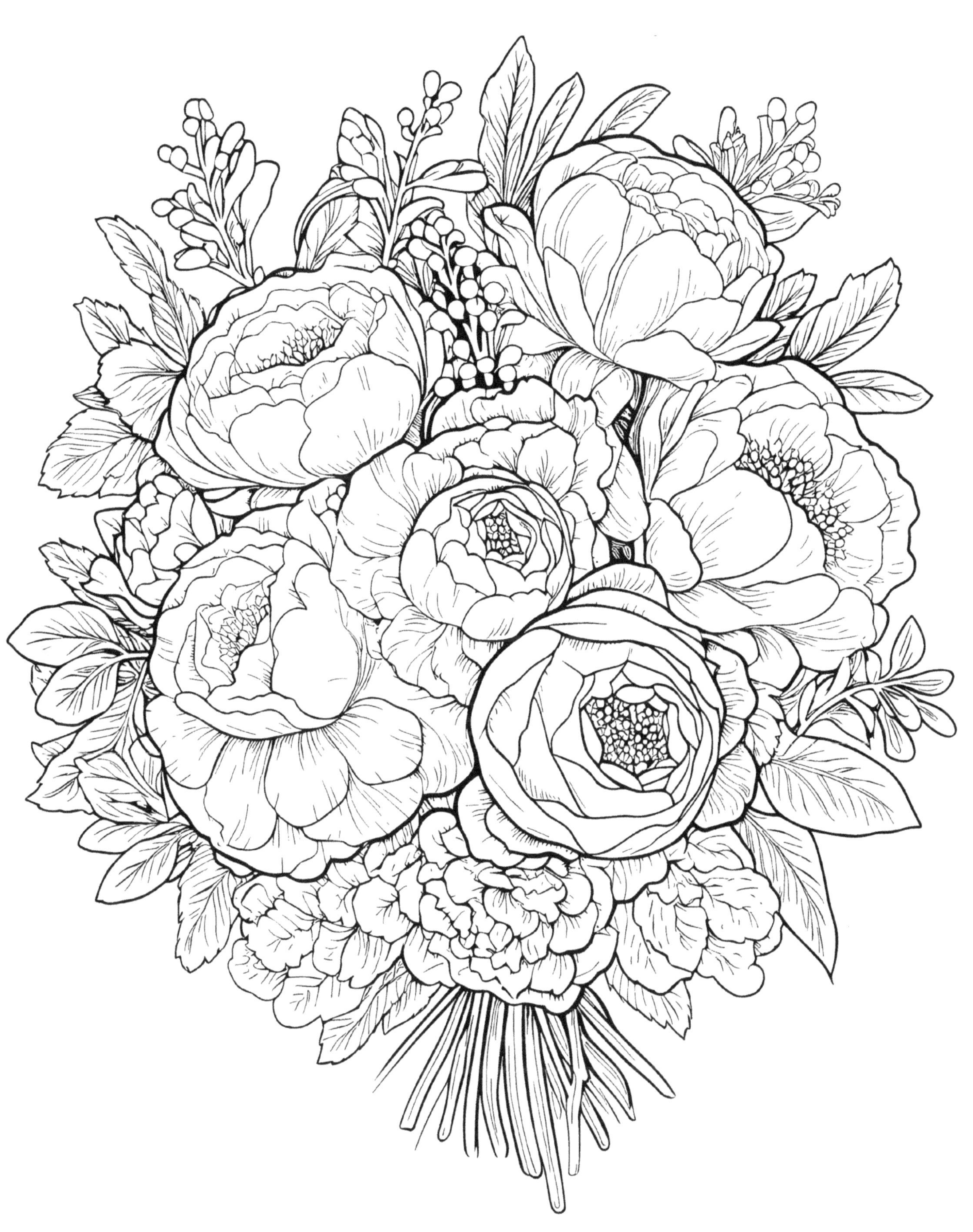

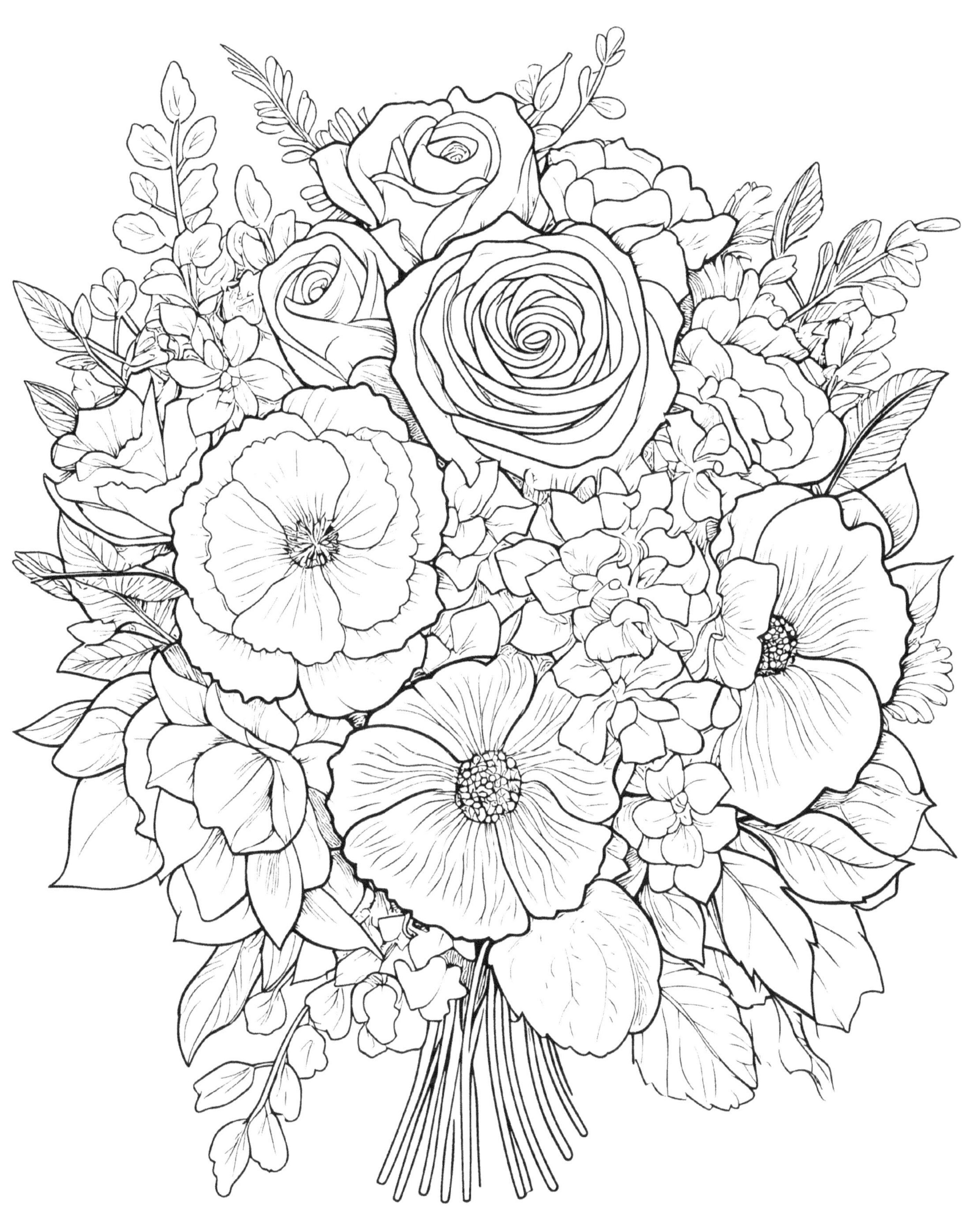

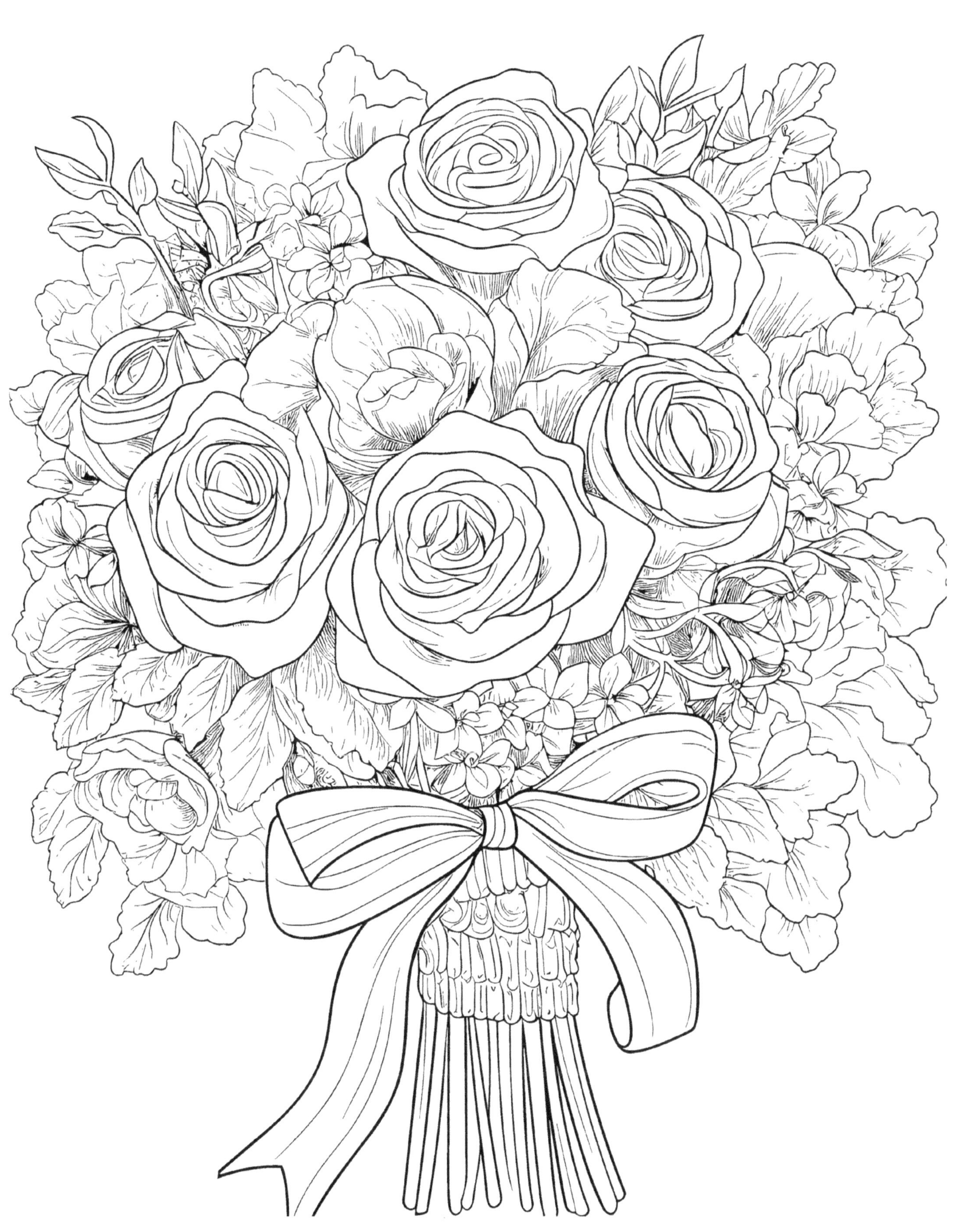

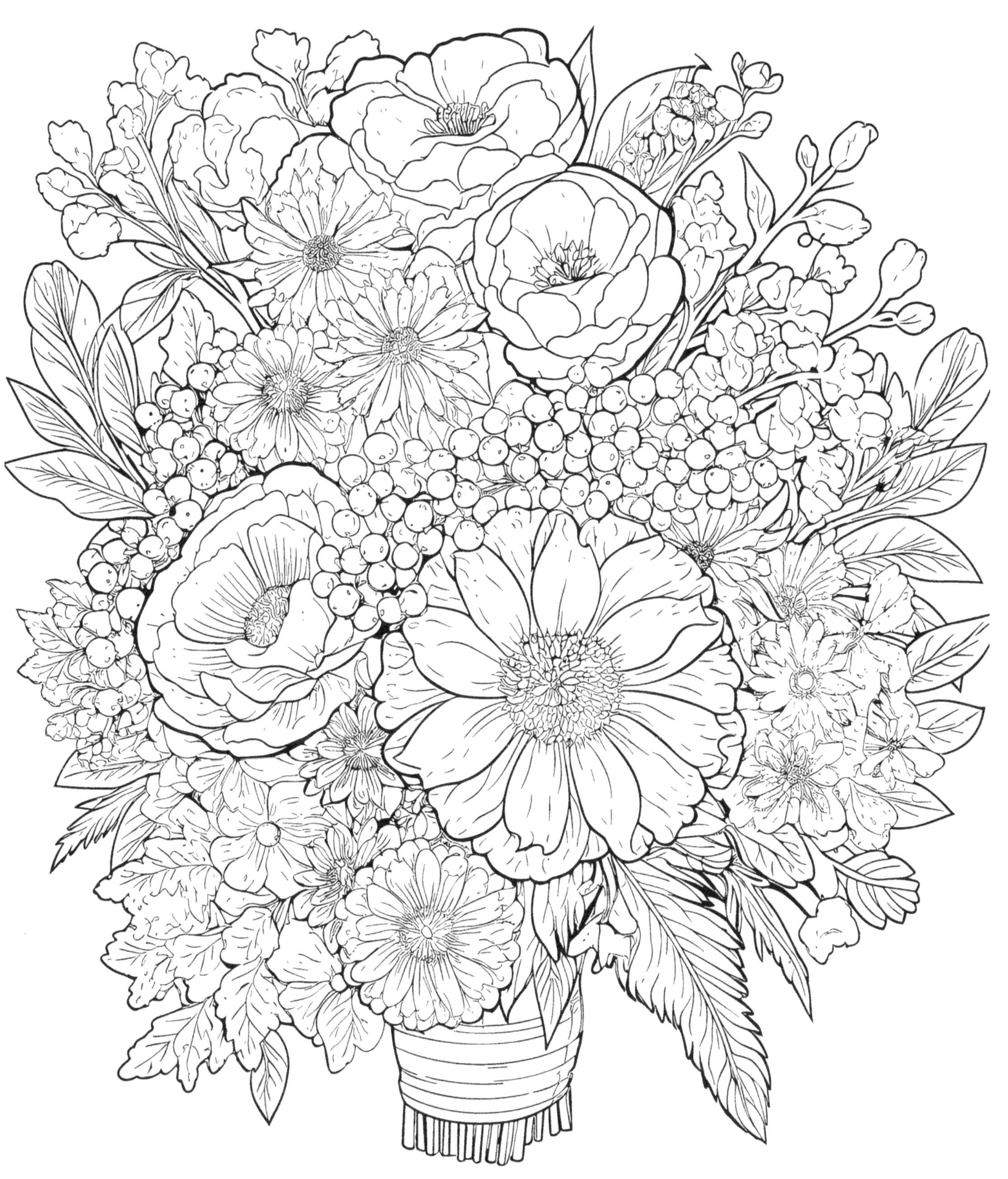

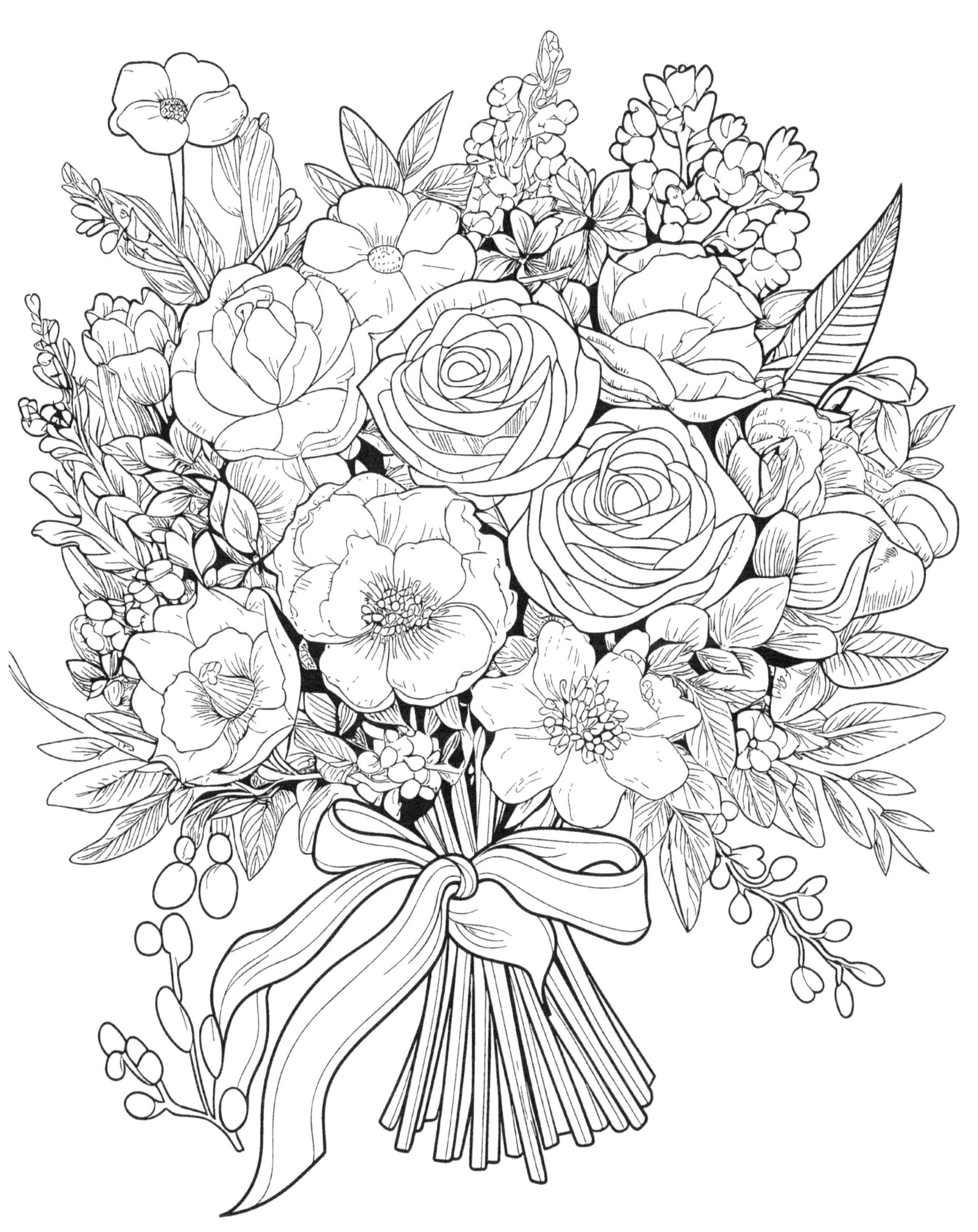

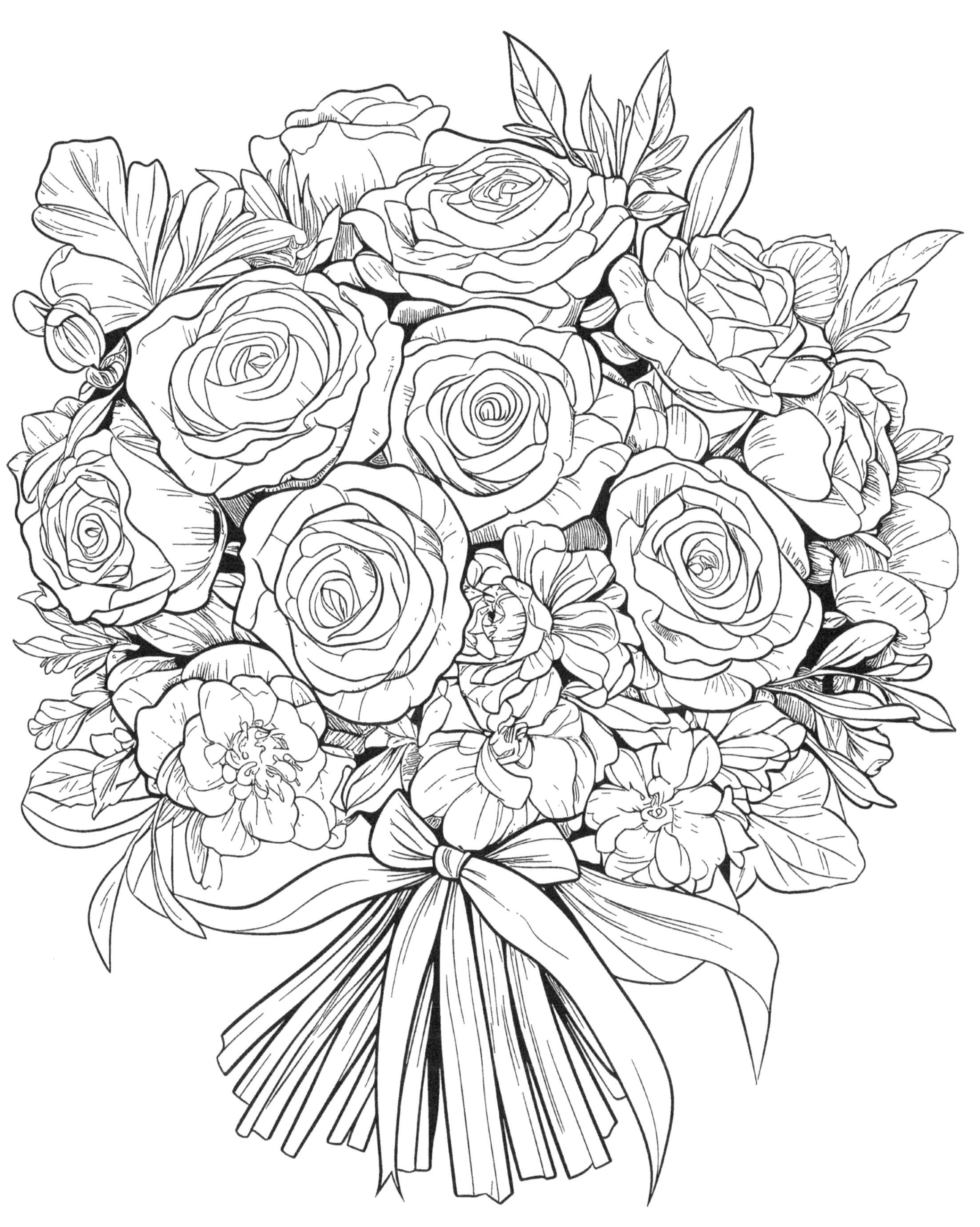

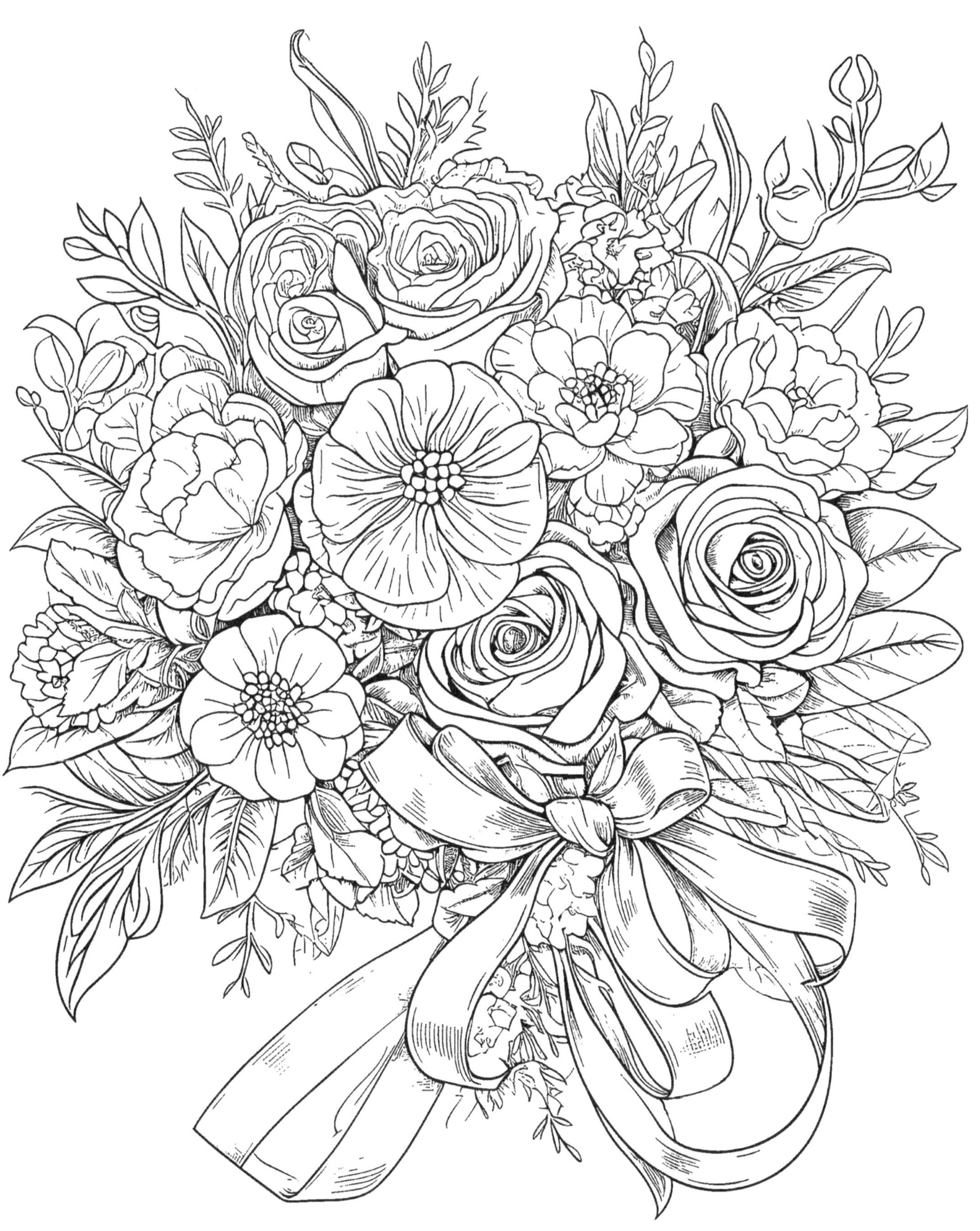

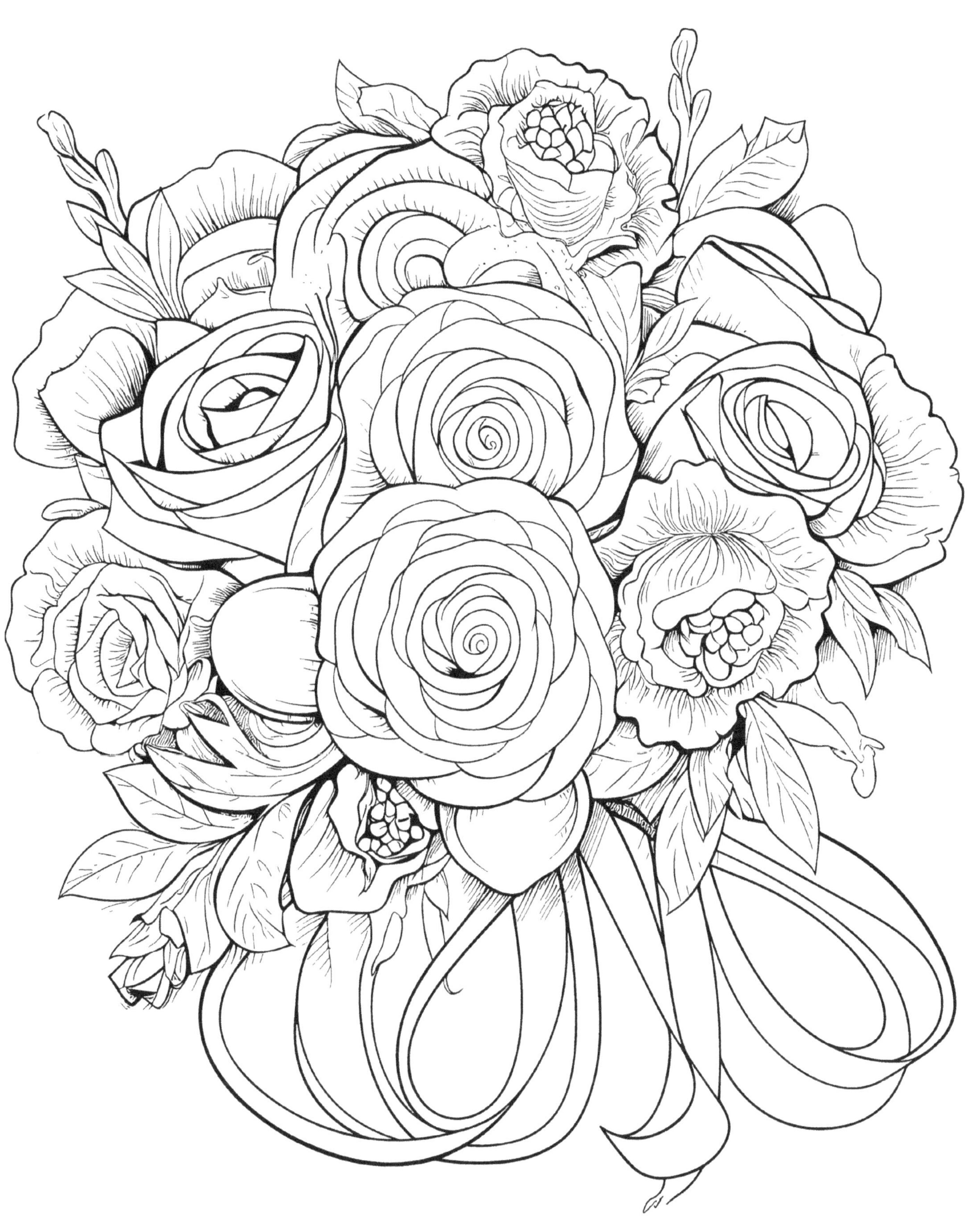

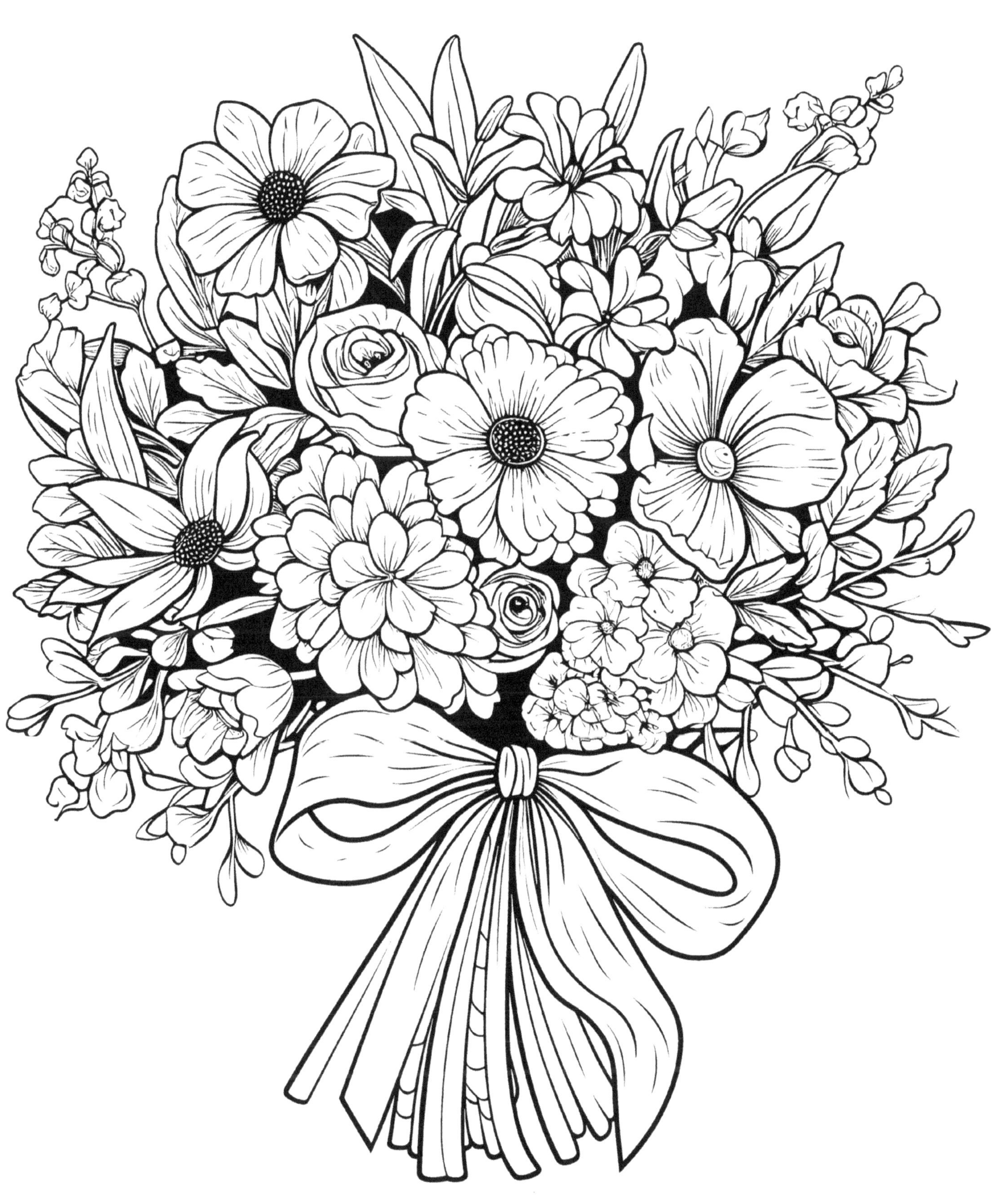

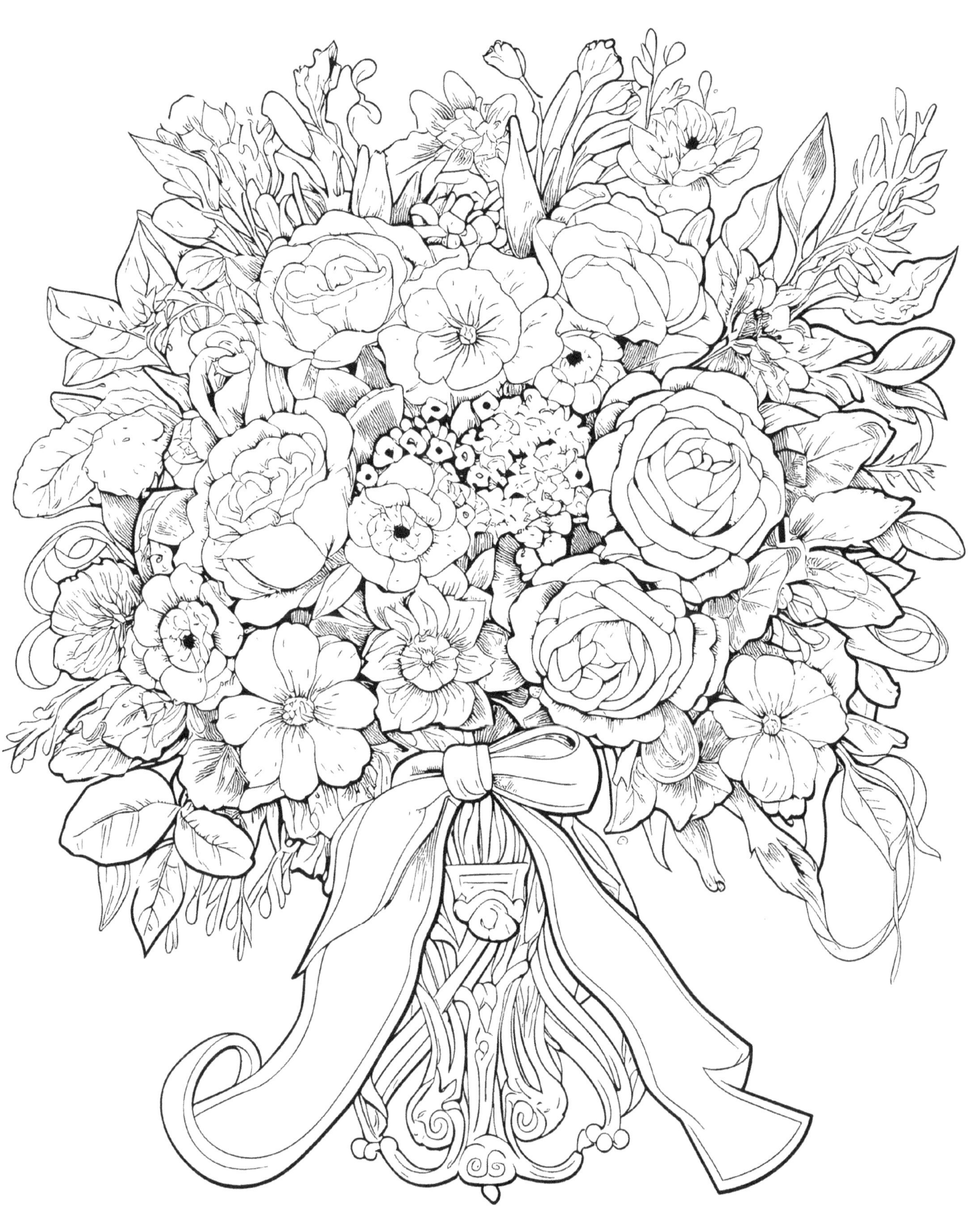

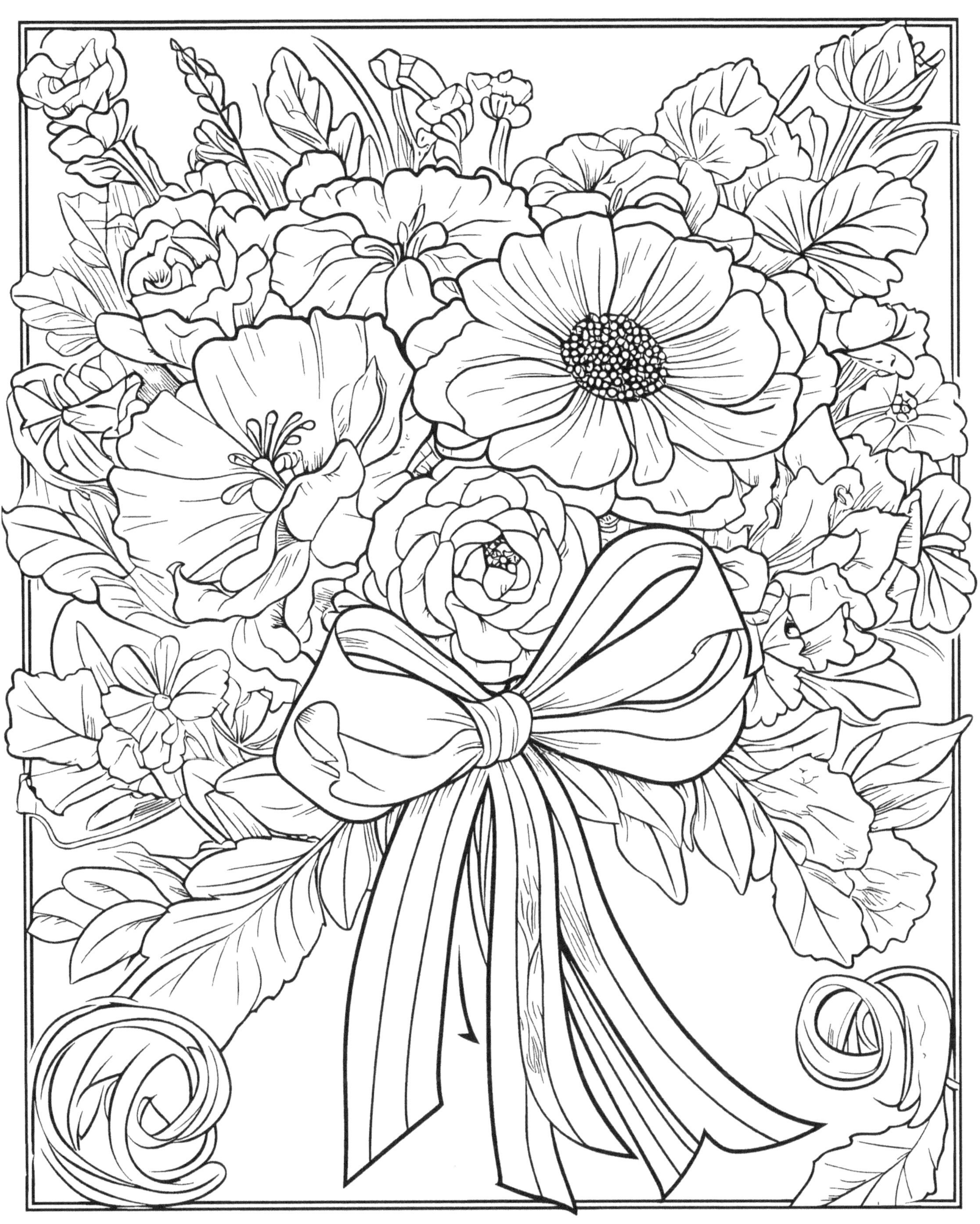

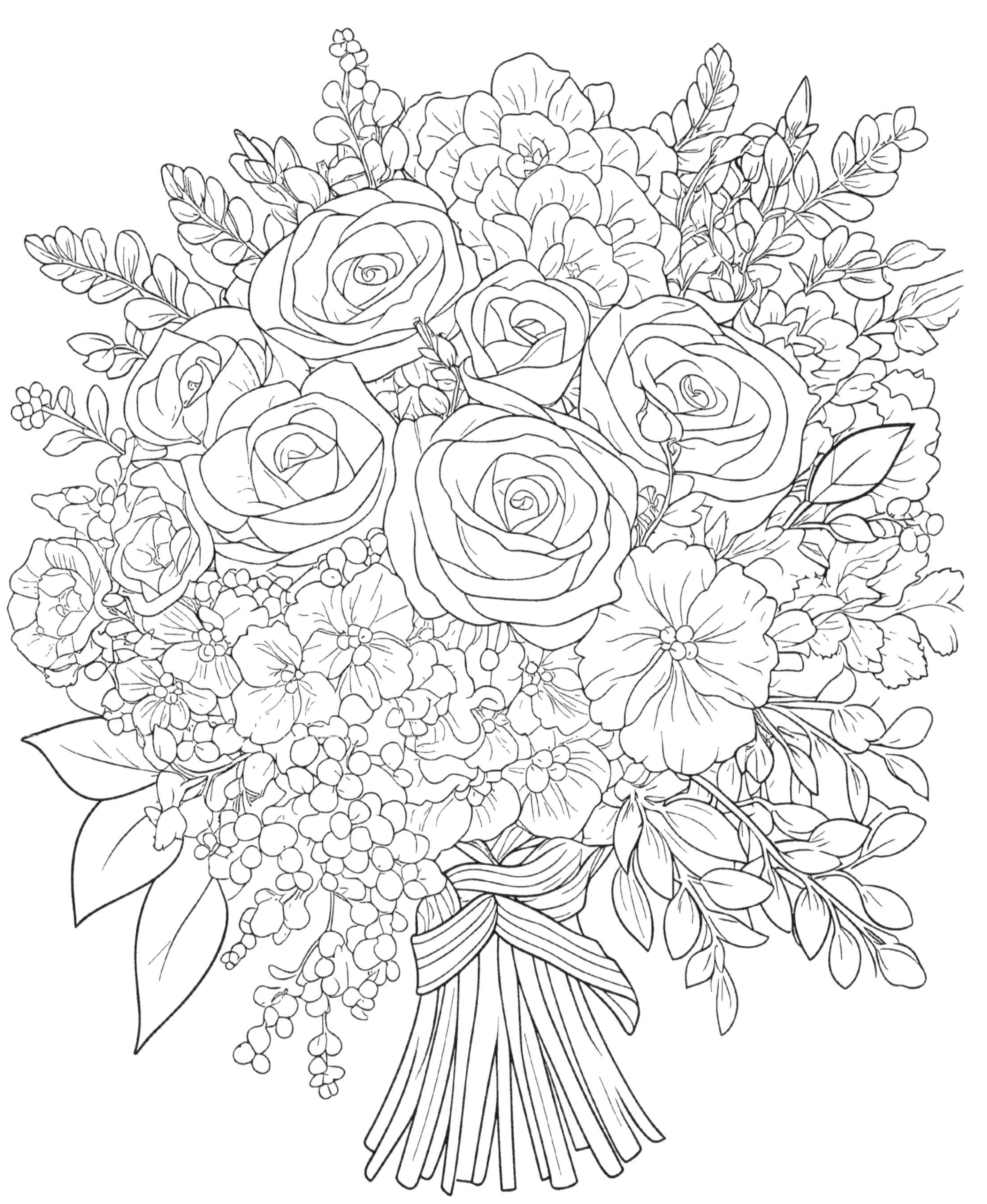

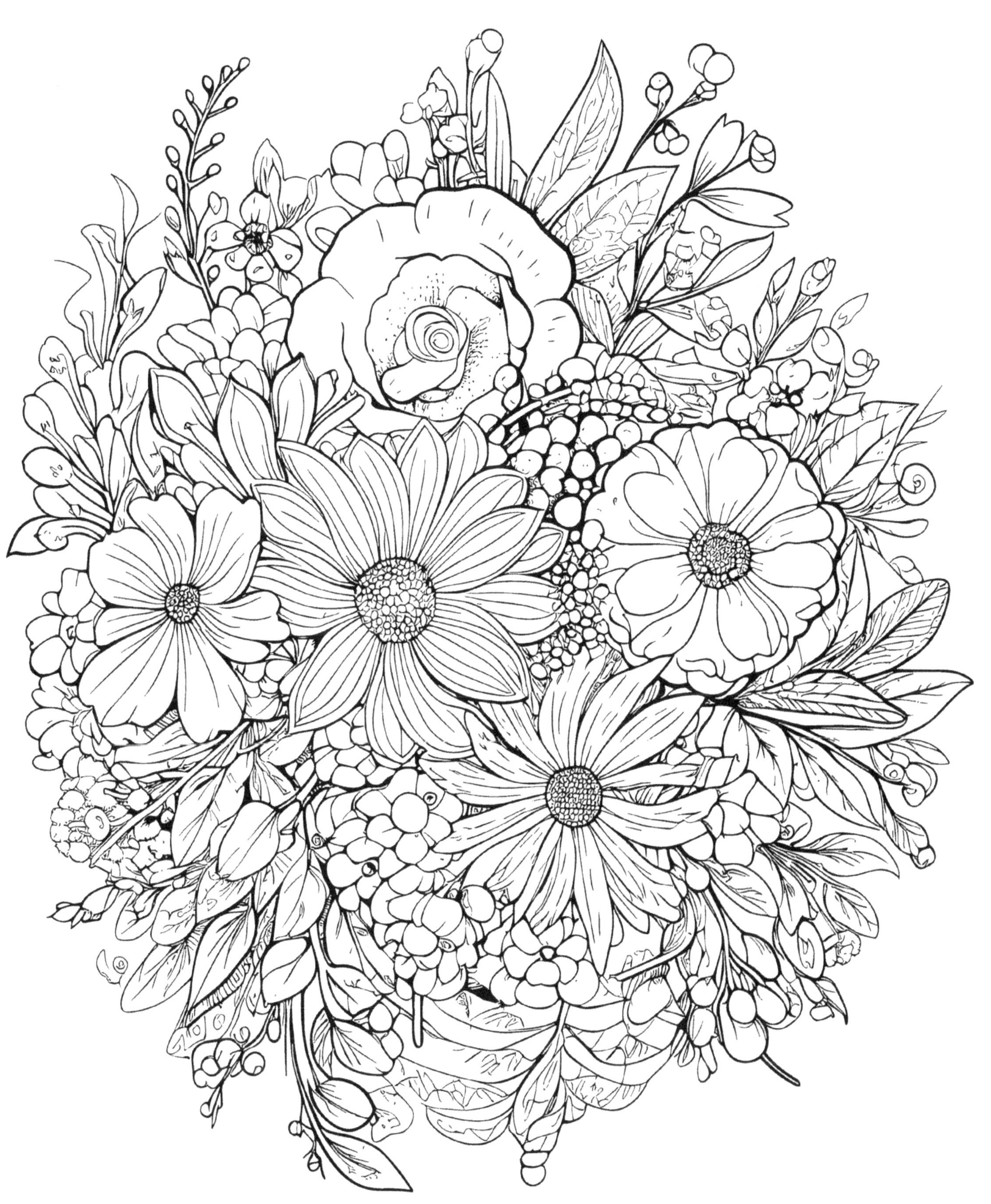

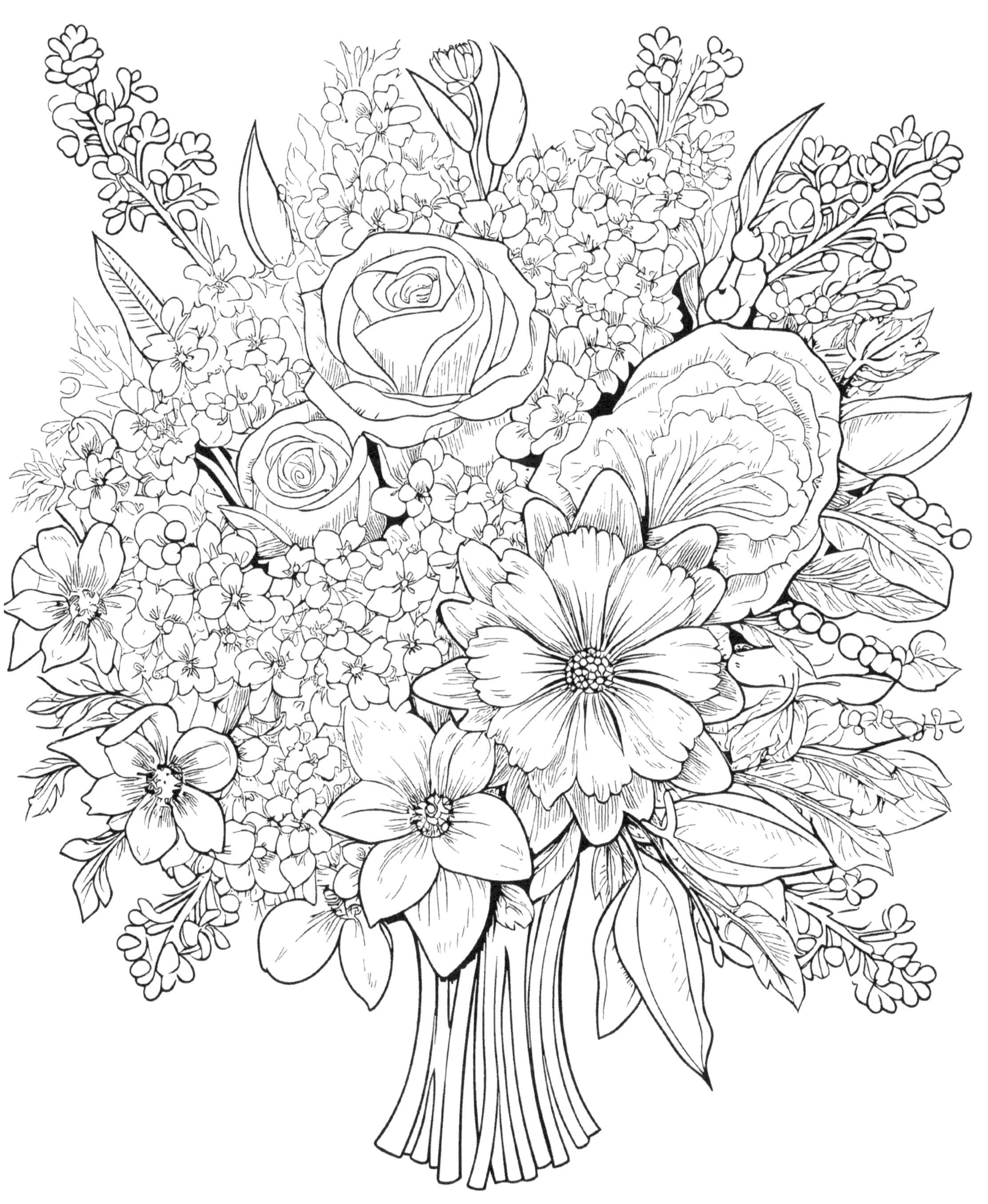

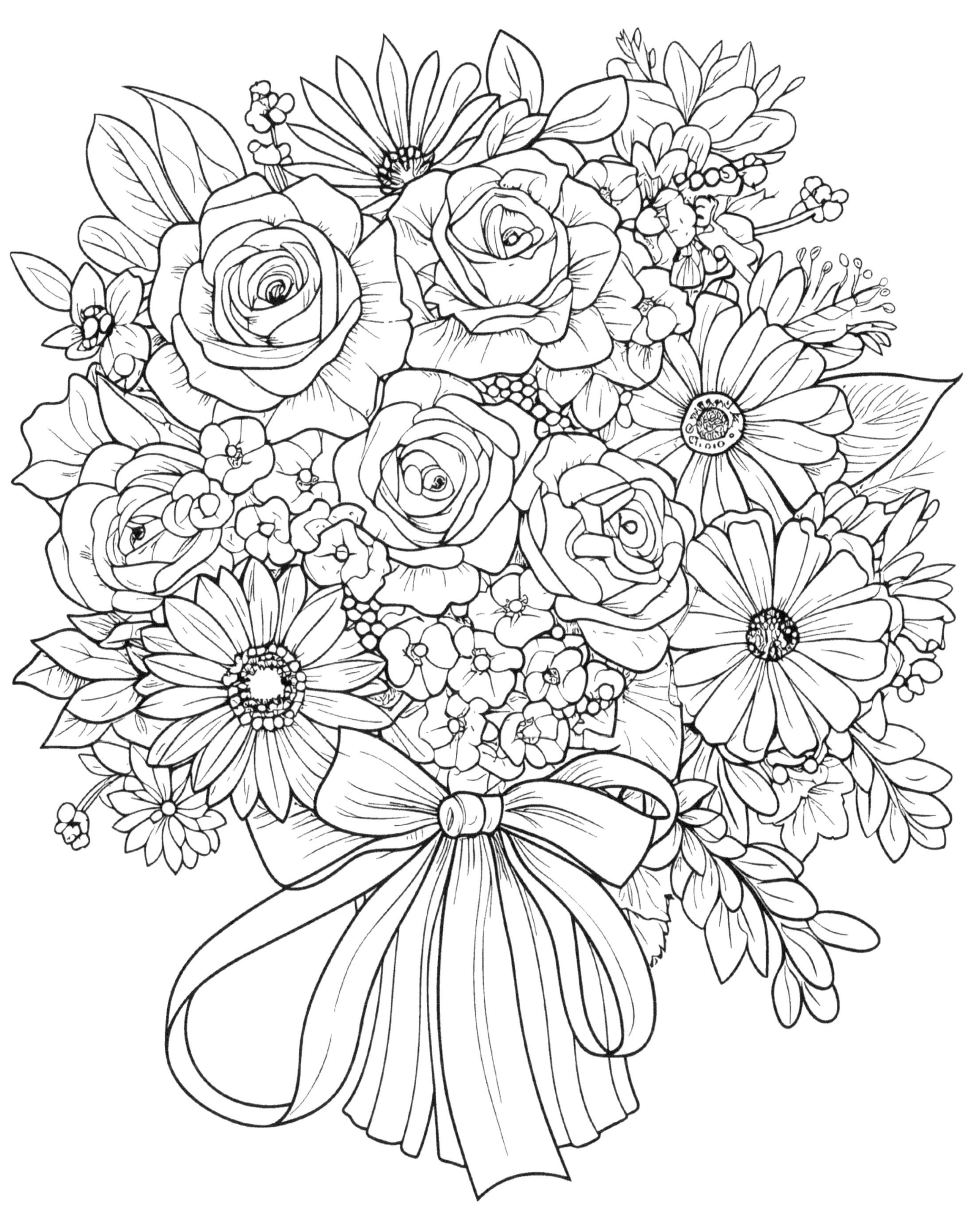

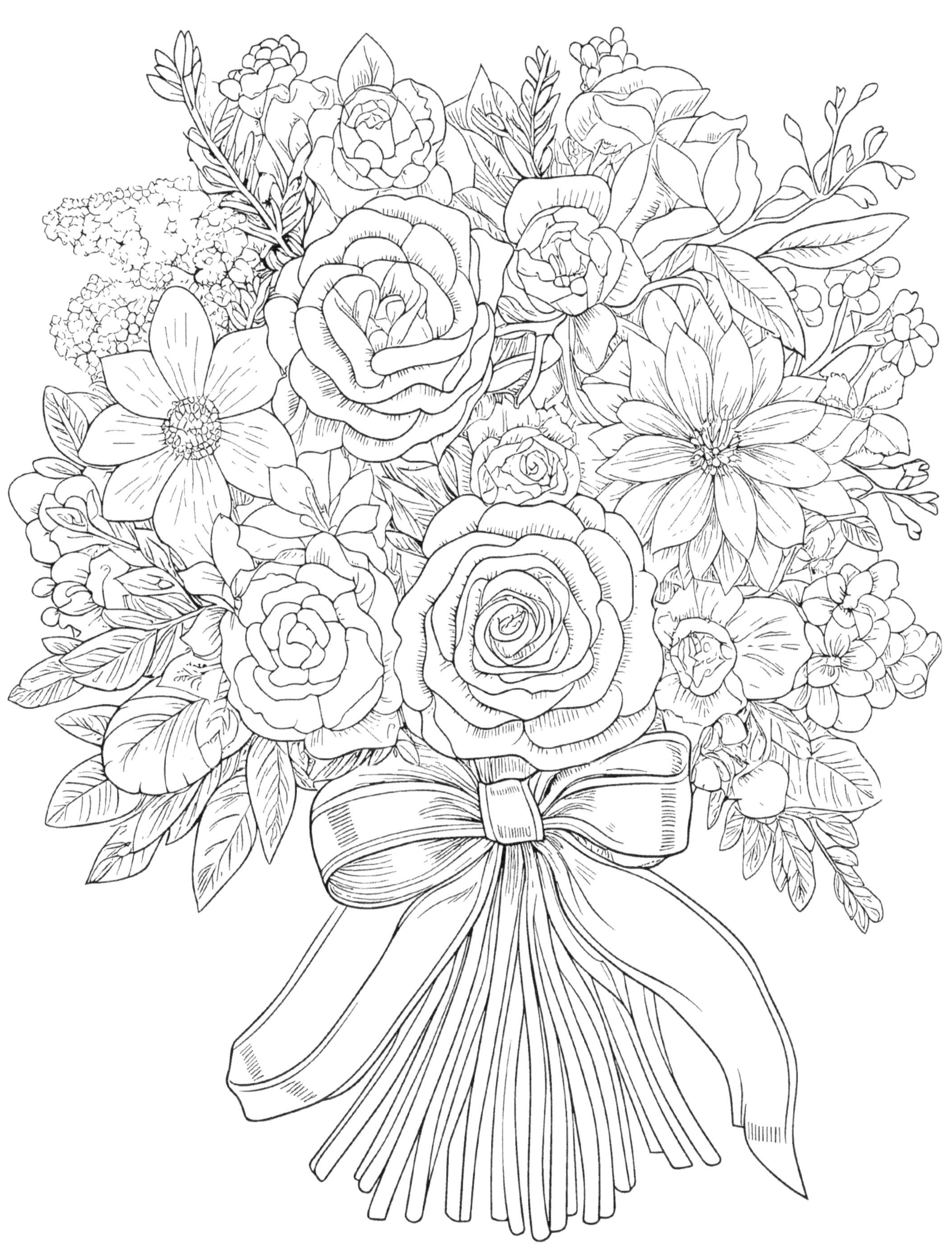

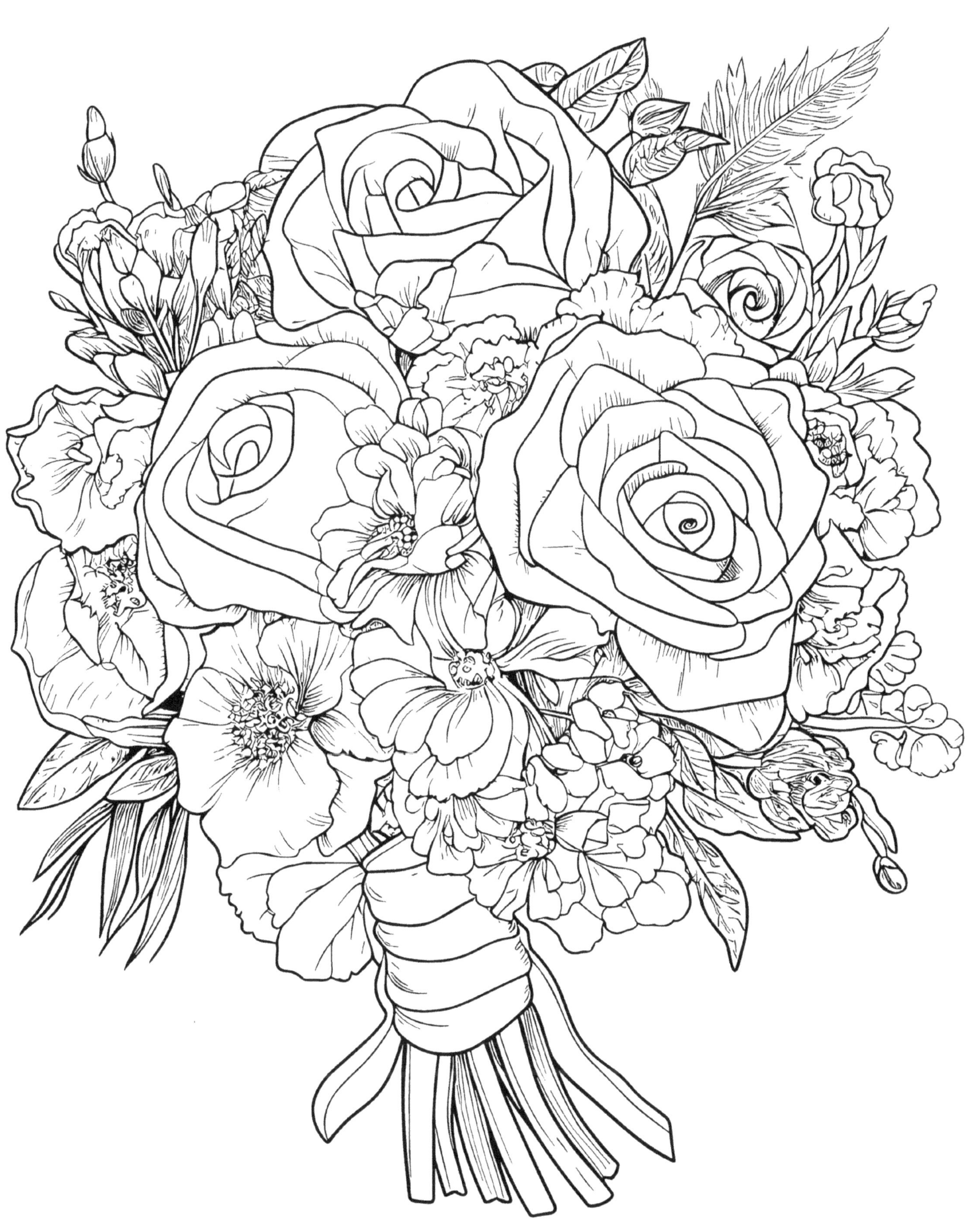

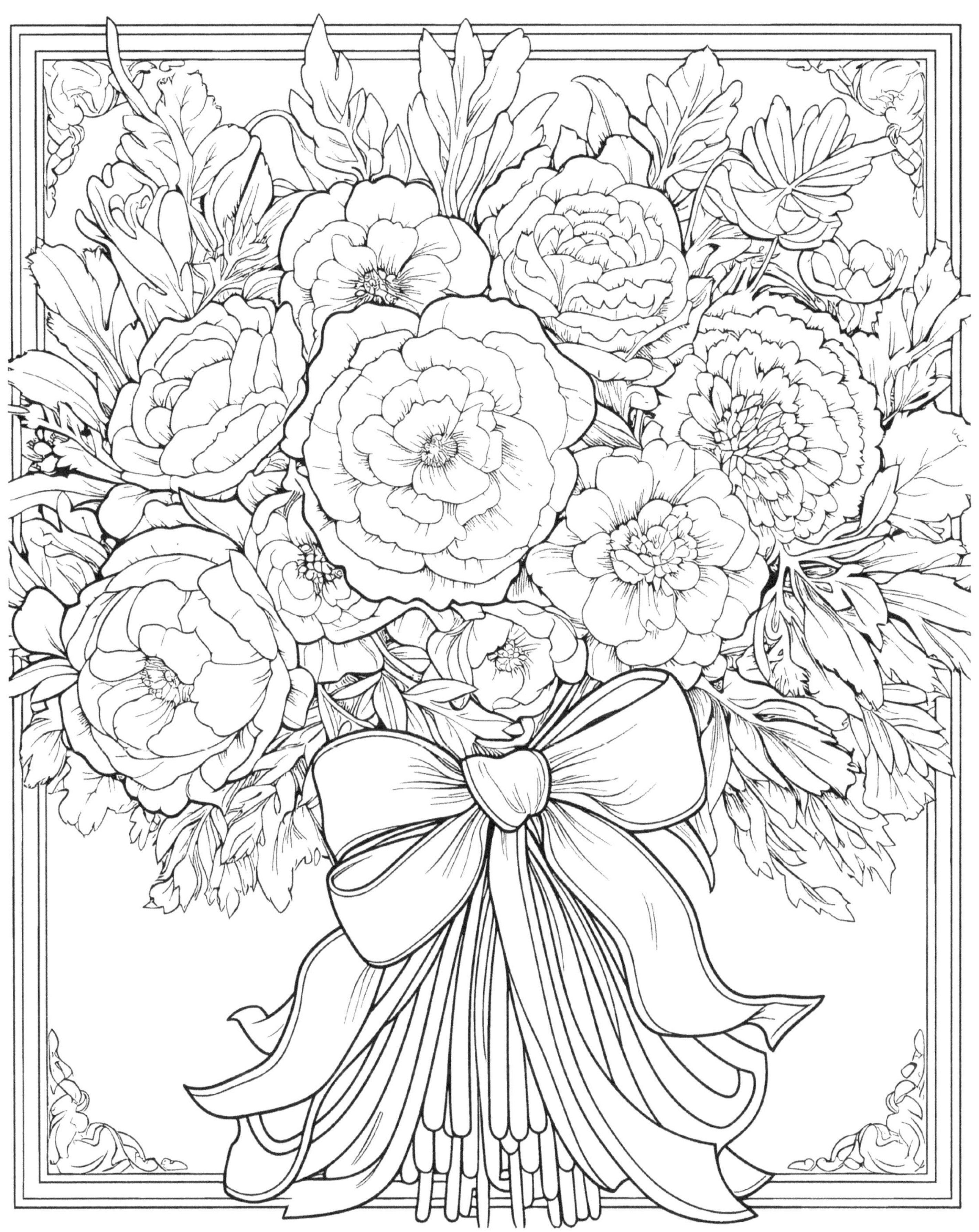

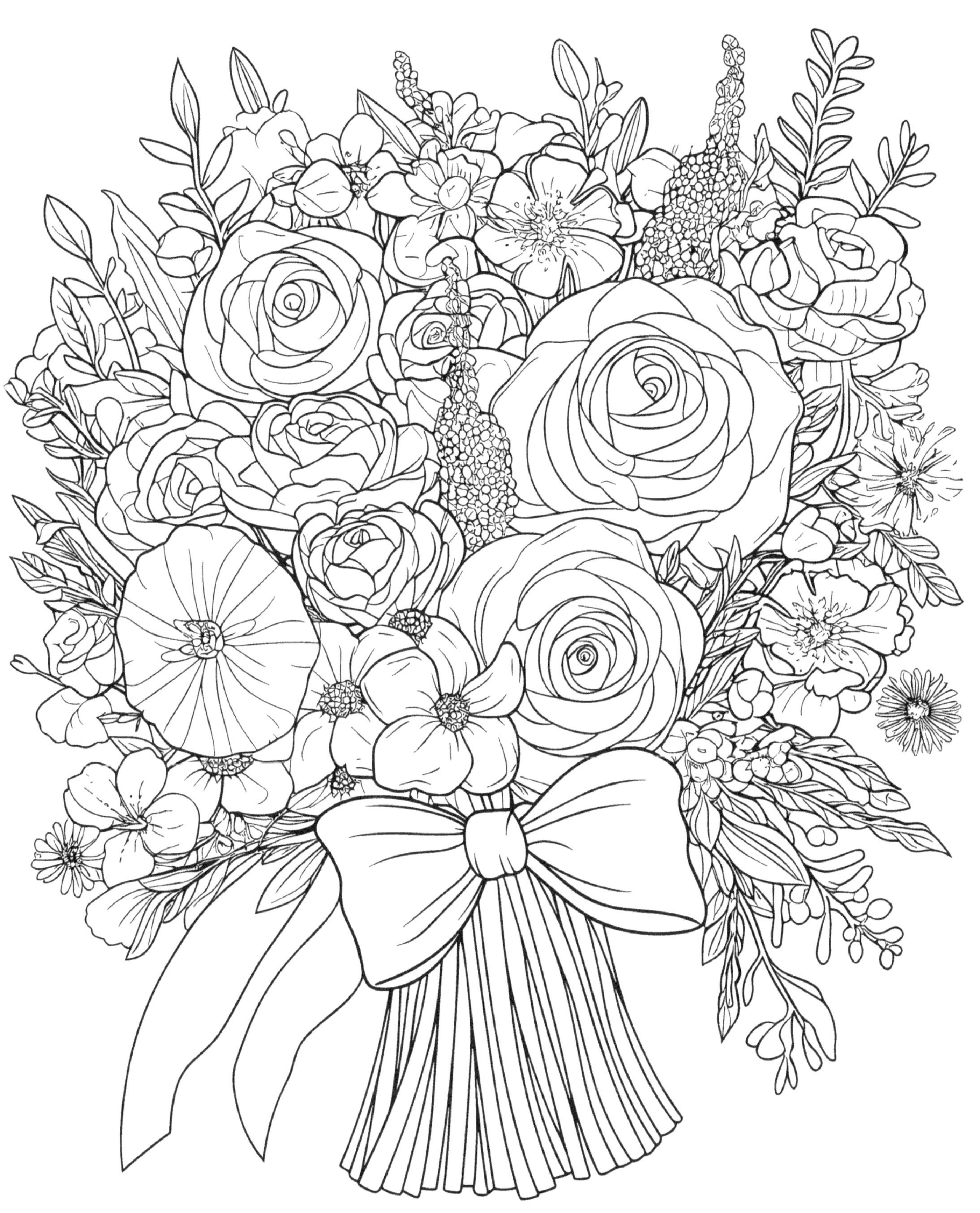

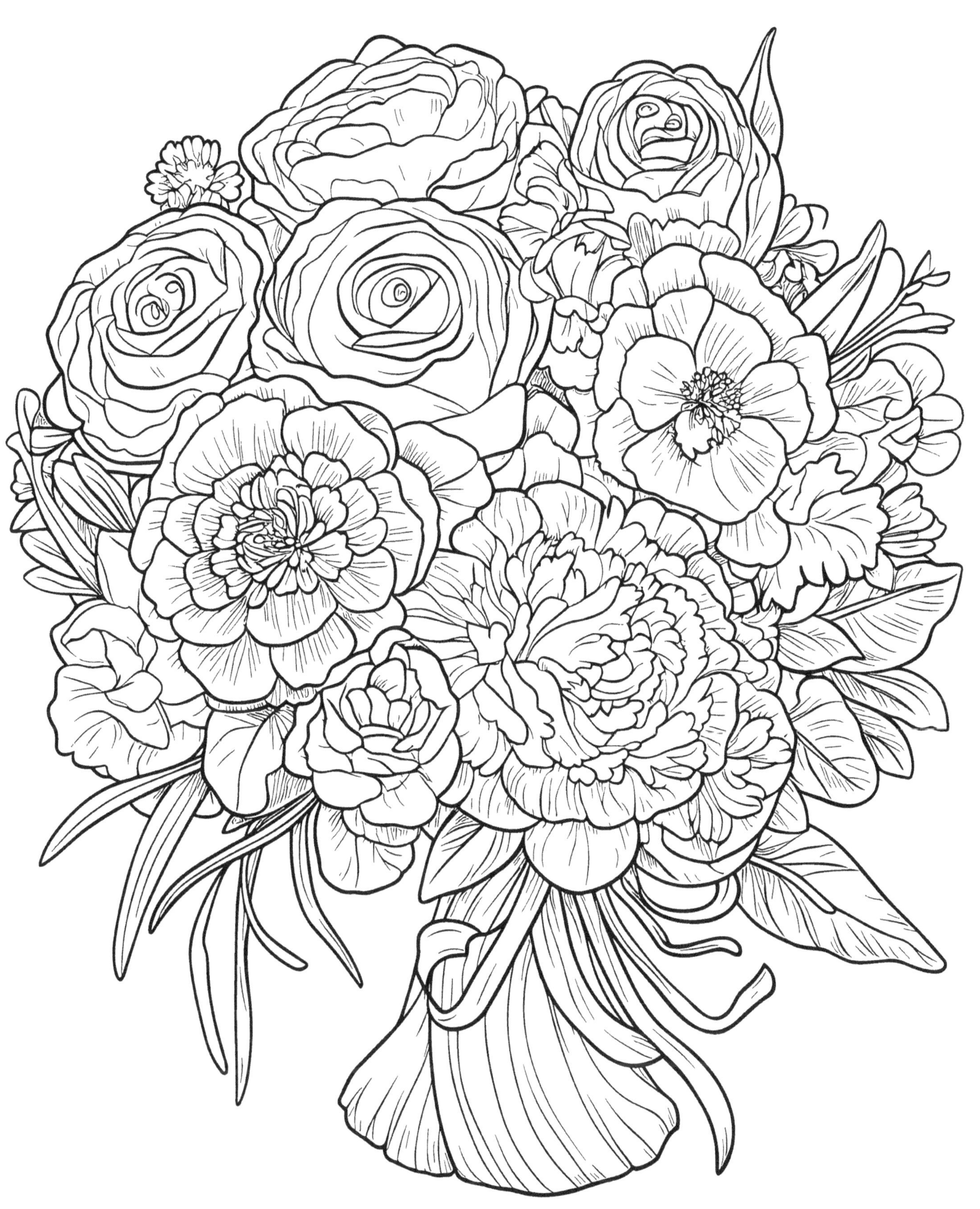

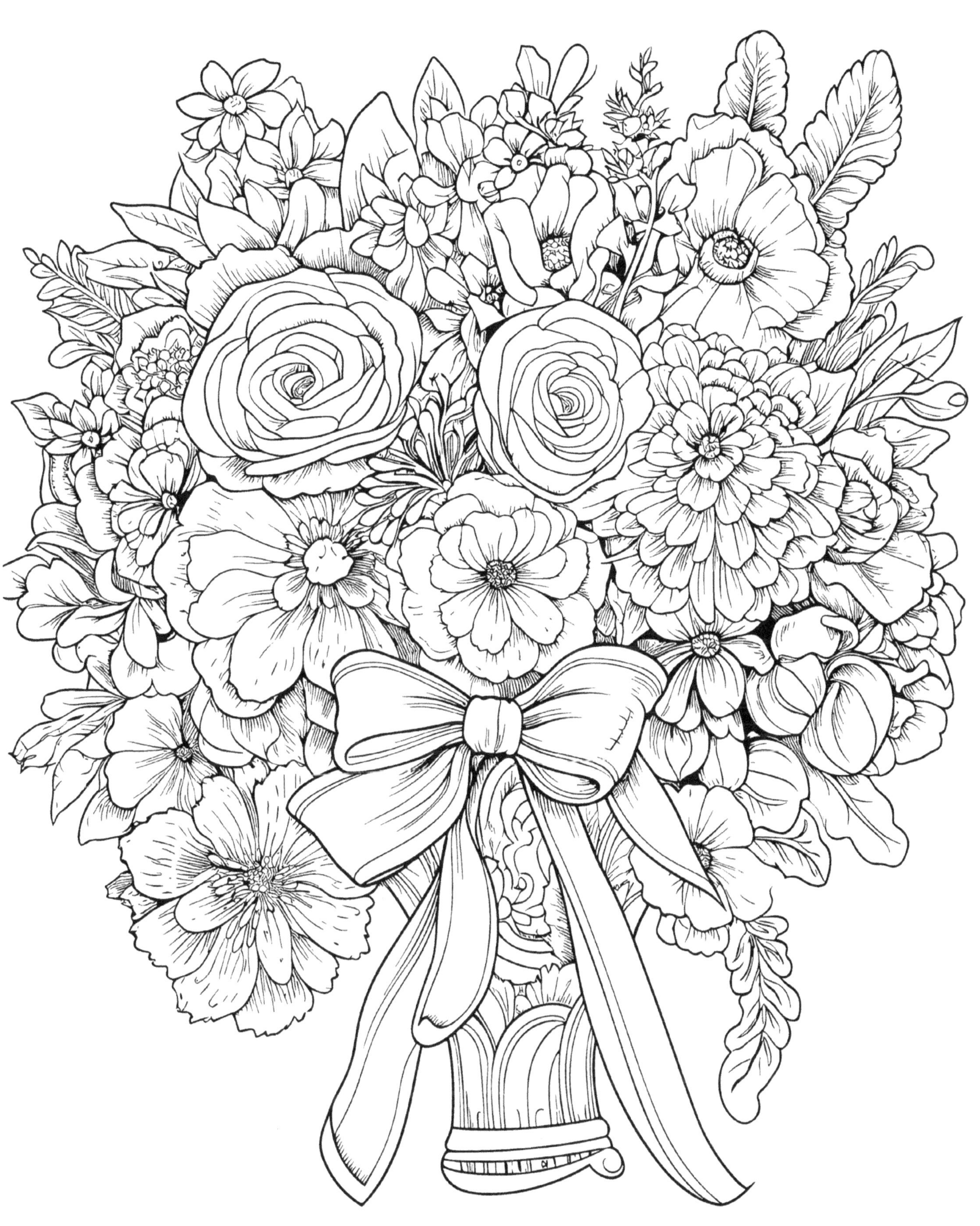

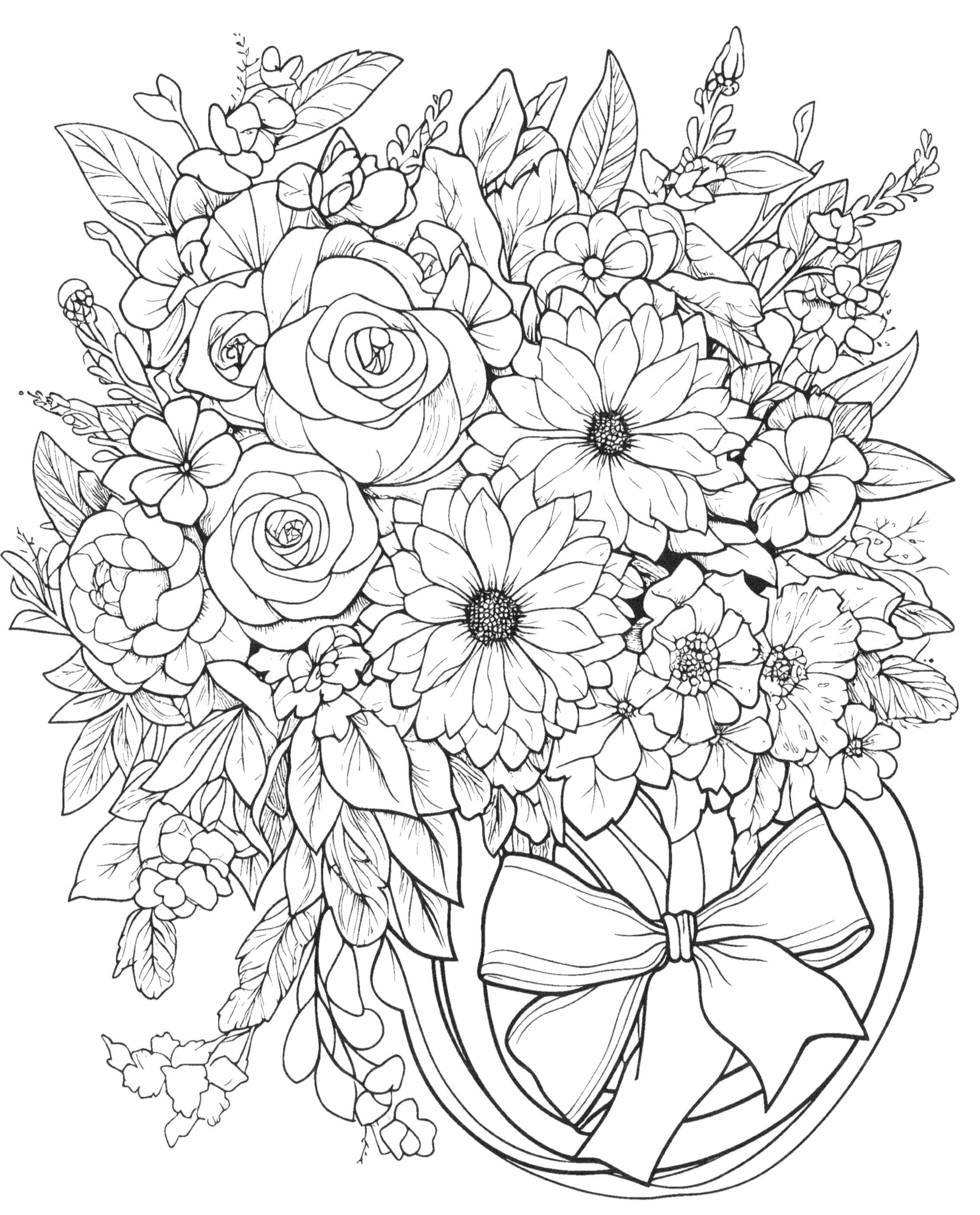

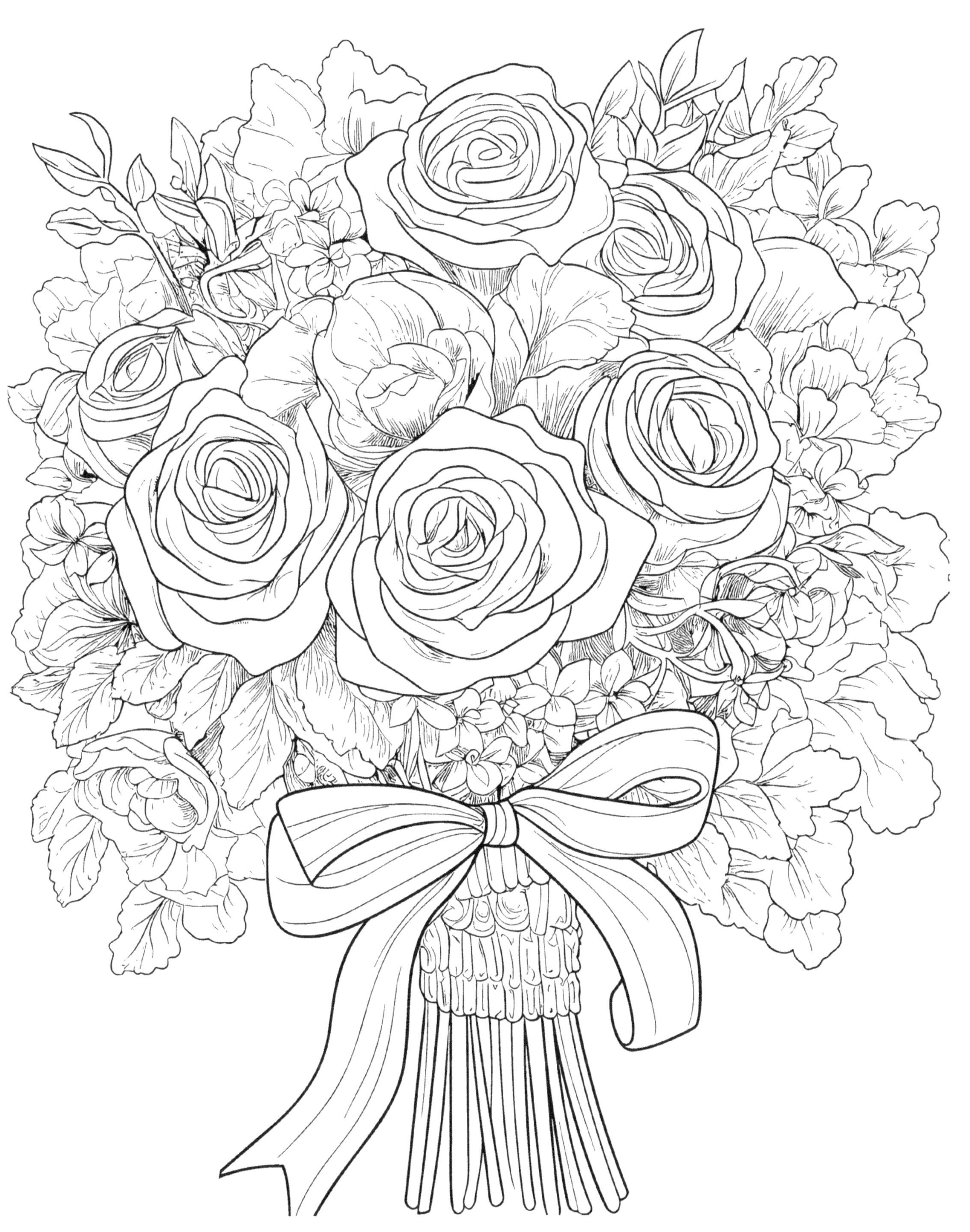

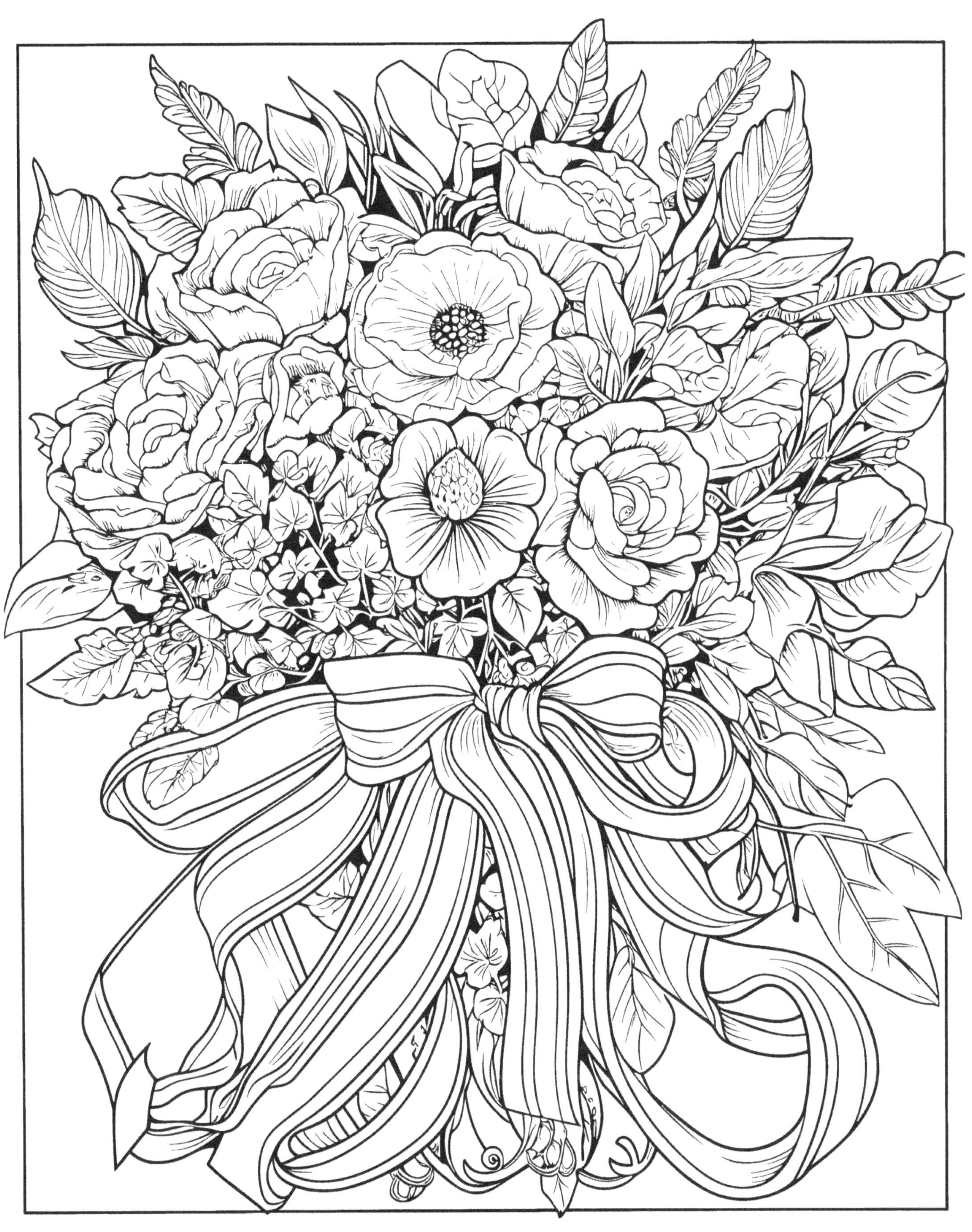

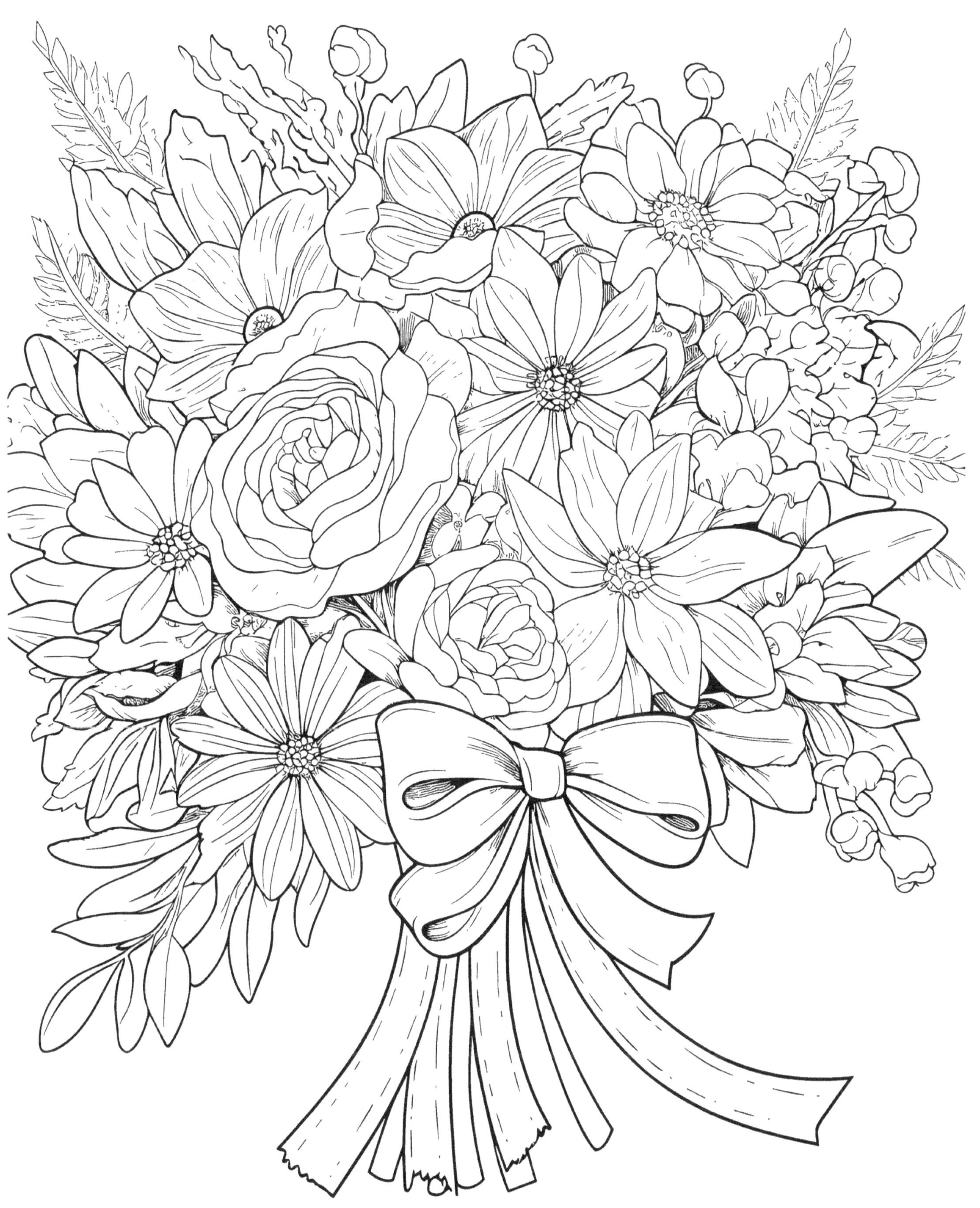

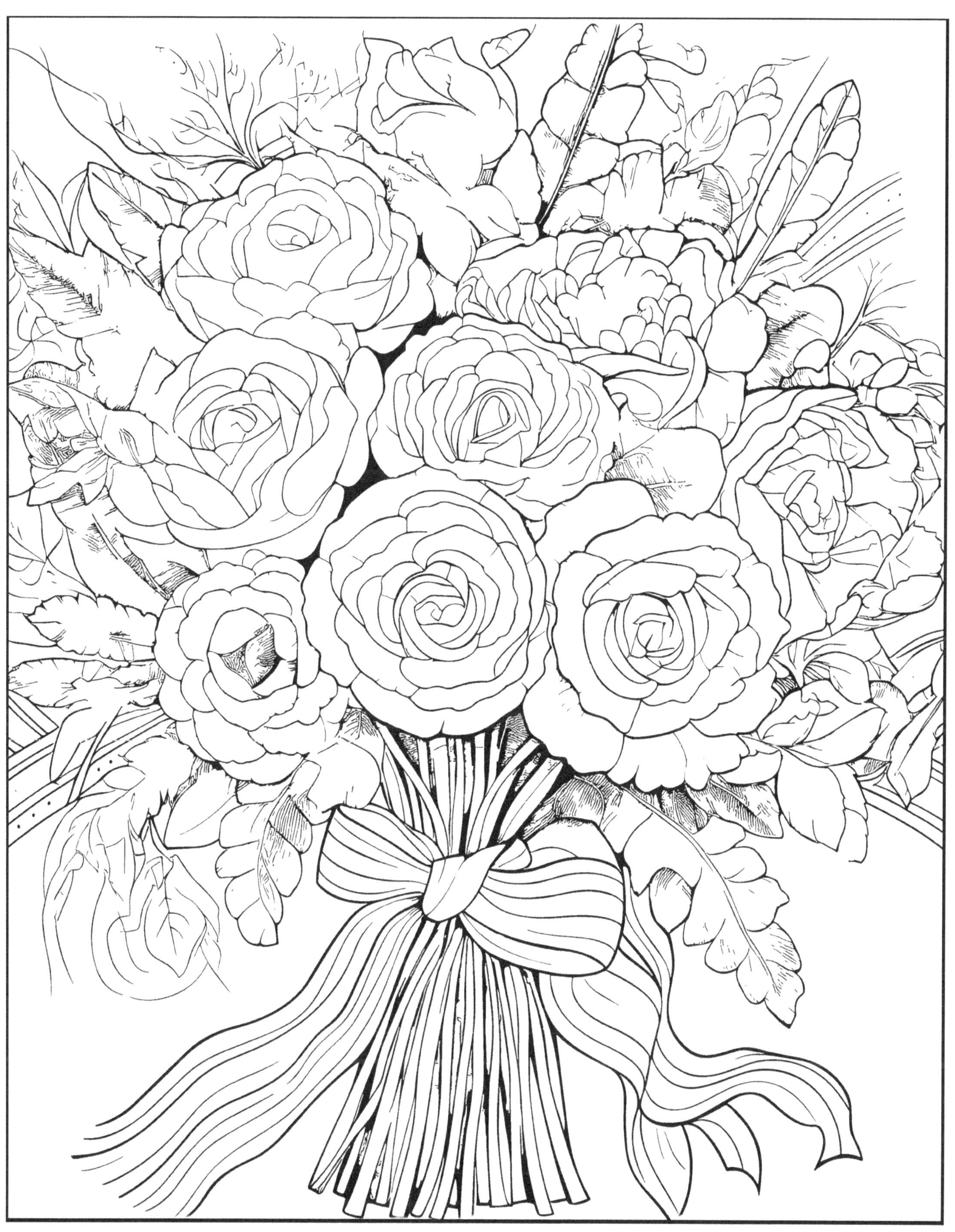

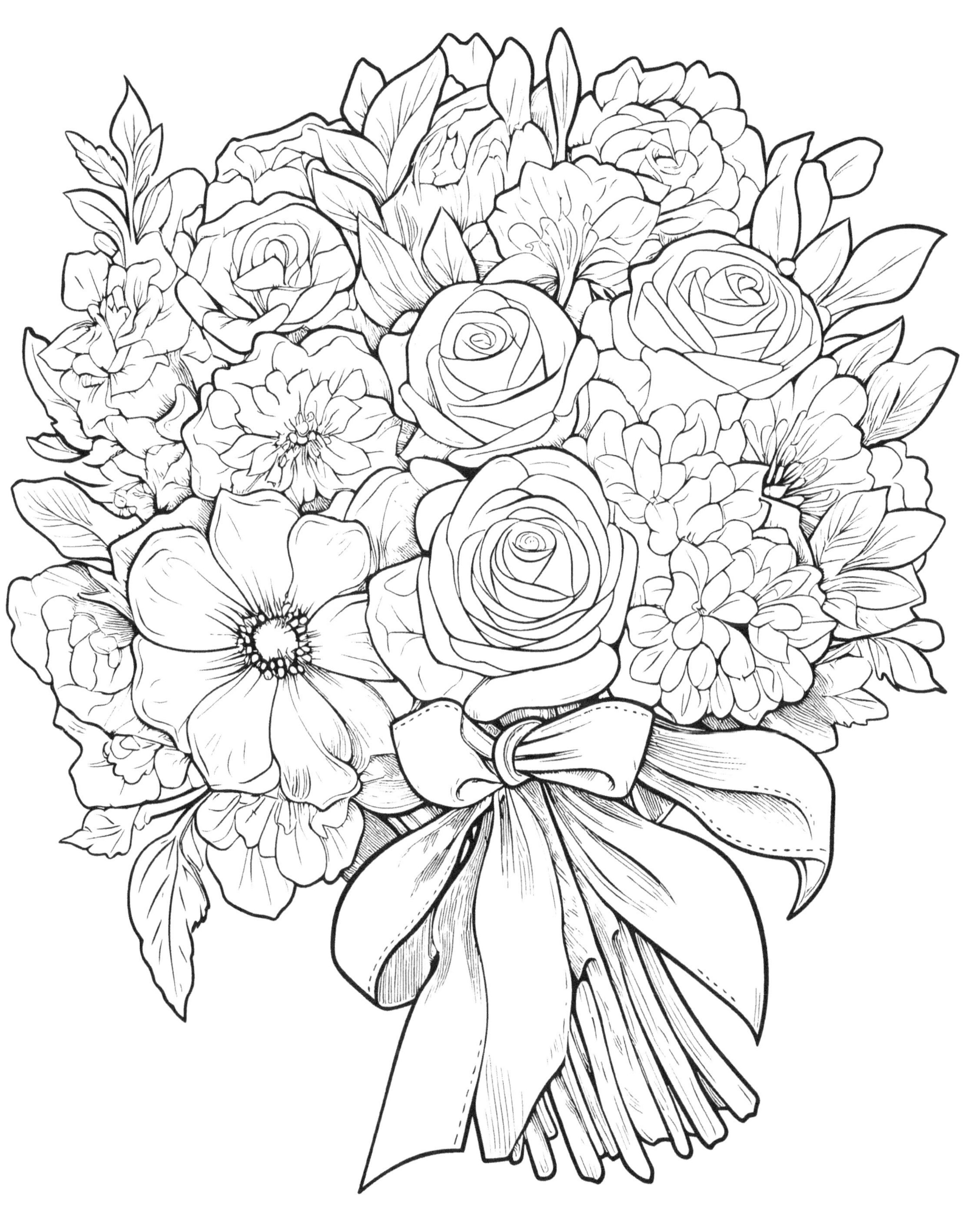

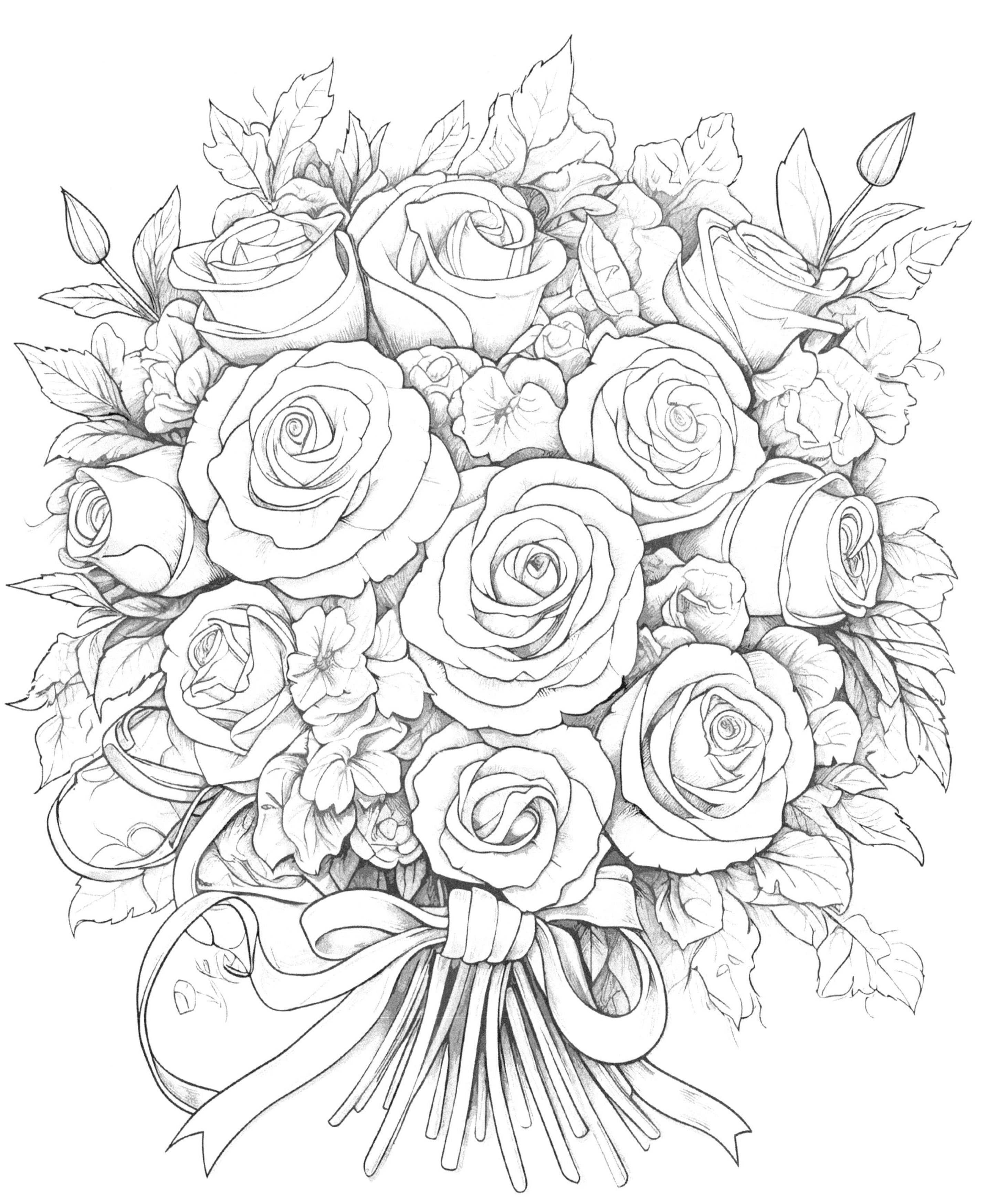

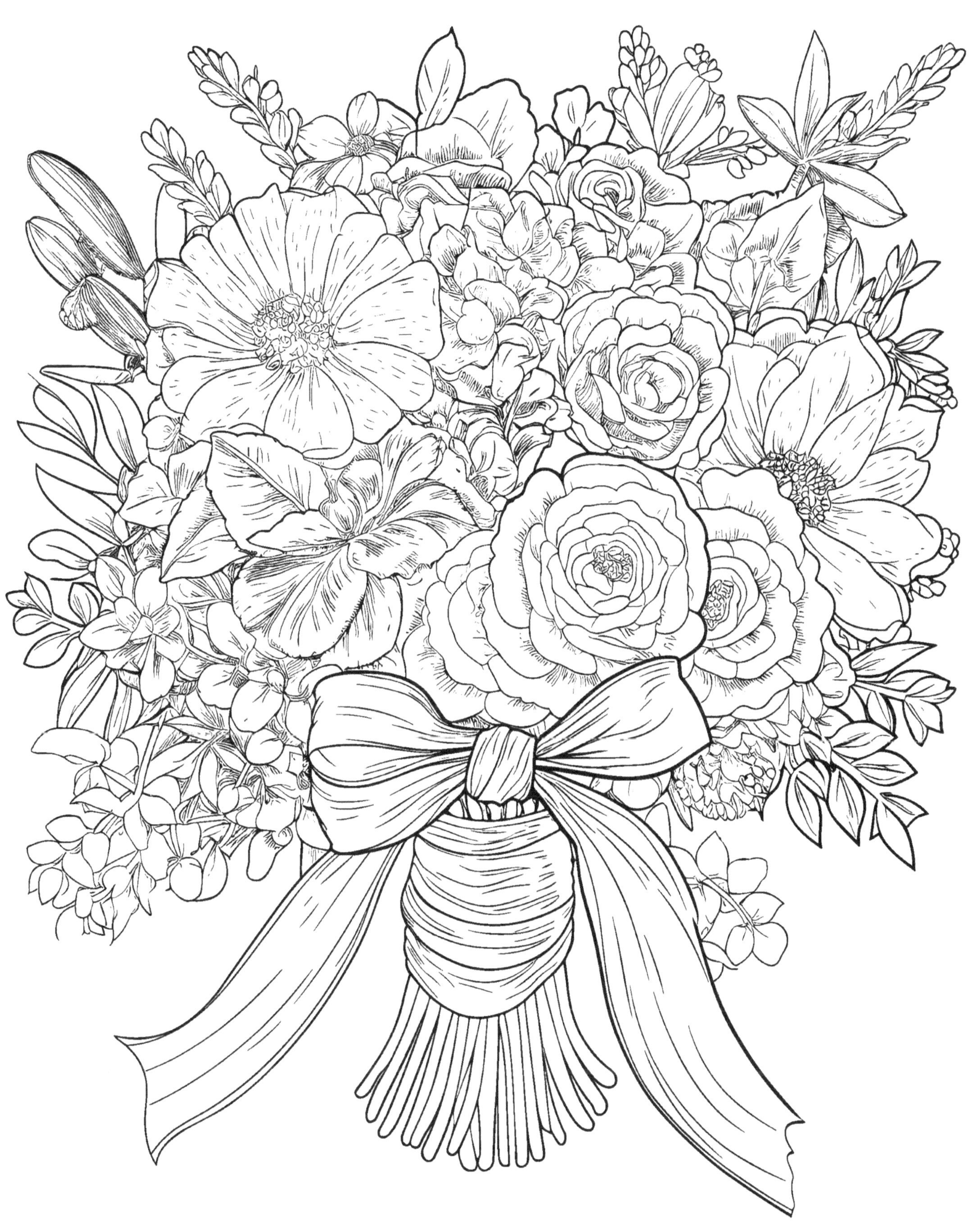

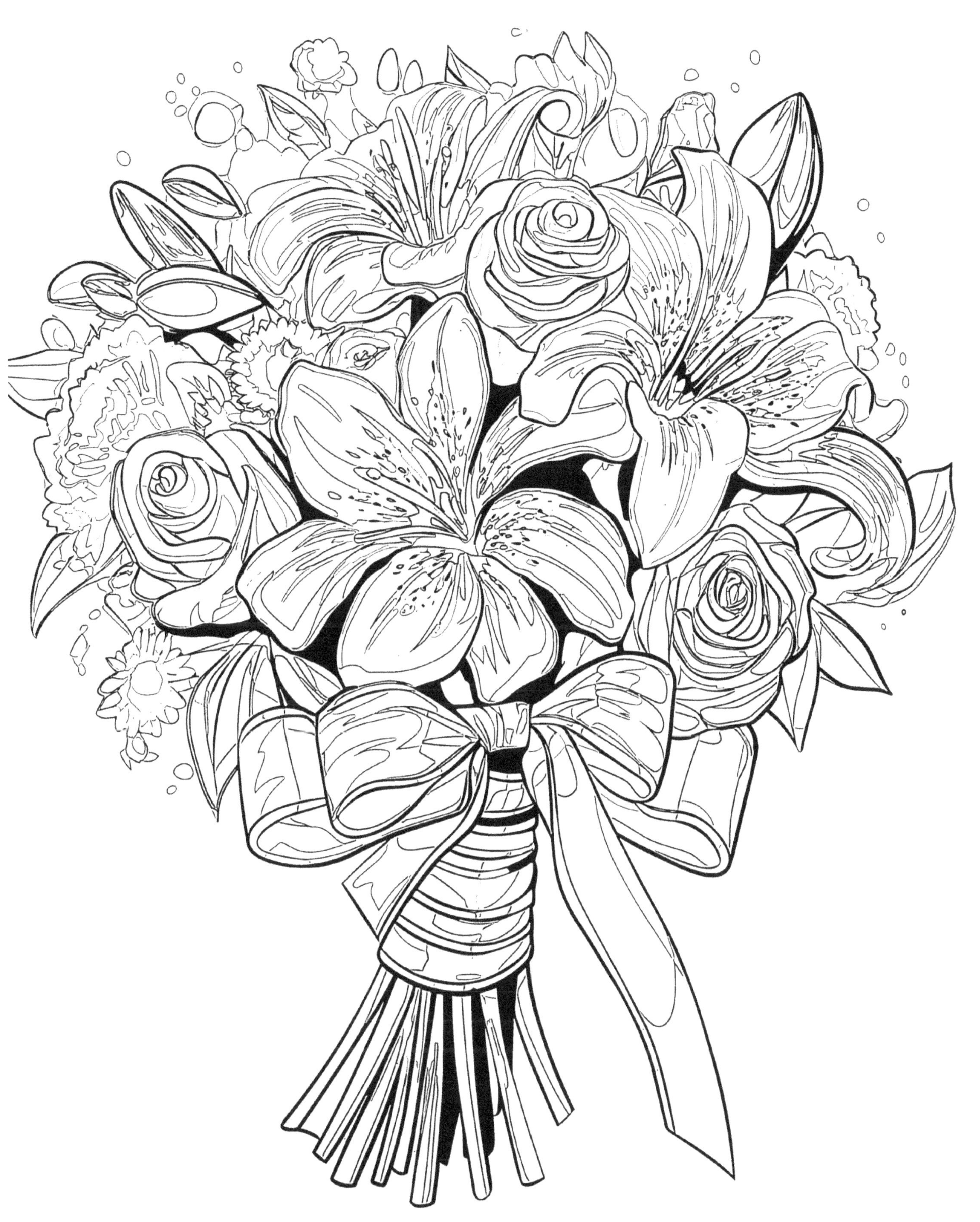

www.ingramcontent.com/pod-product-compliance
Lightning Source LLC
Chambersburg PA
CBHW041038050726
47599CB00018B/1999